# THE SAGE
### AND
# THE GREMLIN

# THE SAGE
## AND
# THE GREMLIN

How to Conquer the World
(Without Thinking Too Hard)

A MEMOIR

## MATT NINER

BLUE MEADOW

BLUE MEADOW

Blue Meadow Press
660 Quince Orchard Road #1011
Gaithersburg, MD 20878

ISBN 979-8-9877908-0-9 (pbk)
ISBN 979-8-9877908-1-6 (ebook)

First paperback printing, November 2023

Certain names and identifying details in this book have been changed to protect the privacy of individuals and organizations.

Cover design by: Colourstreak
connect@colourstreak.com

Originally published in the United States by
Blue Meadow Press, 2023
ISBN 979-8-9877908-0-9

*For Caro, Abi, and Ray –*
*Living proof it was all worth it.*

# CONTENTS

To the mind that is still, the whole universe surrenders.
– Lao Tzu


It's just a ride.
– Bill Hicks

# BIG NEWS

I sat at a white plastic table across from two recruiters, one Japanese and one Canadian, both playing the role of ten-year-old English students. It was my job to teach these two pretend children the difference between the words *for* and *since* when talking about the passage of time. I'd already convinced myself that this company would never, ever hire me, so I didn't really give a damn how the interview went. This approach does wonders for the nerves.

"I have lived in America for twenty years!" I began.

"You have twenty-four years?"

"No, not *four* for... I mean *for* for."

Blank stares.

"Okay... I live in America now, right?"

"Yes. You are American."

"Good. So, let's say I was born in 1982," I said, writing the year on the left side of the whiteboard behind me. "Now it's 2002." I drew a big 2-0-0-2 on the right. "This whole time," I continued, tracing a line between the two years, "I have lived in America. This is twenty years. I have lived in America *for* twenty years."

Just then one of them muttered something to the other in Japanese. Her colleague responded in kind, and they both turned back to me.

"I understand," they said in unison.

"Good!" I plowed forward. "So when we use *for*, that's the total duration of time. Twenty years, in this case. Now, I can also say that I've lived in America *since* 1982." I pointed at the year again and circled it. "With *since*, I use the time when I first started living in America. The moment I began living in America."

Blank stares.

In six minutes the exercise was over and my students switched back to adult mode. It wasn't a train wreck, but it was pretty clear I'd only ever given passing thought to this basic grammatical concept. When they asked me to rate my performance on a scale of zero to ten, I gave myself a five.

"So, you think you could have done it better?" the Canadian asked.

"Oh, absolutely." I turned to her classmate and made a little rocking motion with my hand. "That was only so-so." A minuscule curl appeared at the corner of her mouth as she jotted down some notes. After a few follow-up questions they told me someone would contact me within seven days and thanked me for coming.

I left the room, stepped back into the elevator, and ripped the accursed tie from my neck, leaving the hotel just as I'd walked in – with no hope of a job offer. The blinding sun, chilly air, and ungodly urban soundtrack that attacked my senses brought me crashing back to downtown Boston and I put the interview out of mind. I'd just have to find some other way to see the world. Who wants to be a teacher, anyway? Seven days came and went. My roommates continued their frantic search for employment while I procrastinated, praying for some miracle to deliver me from the 9-to-5 purgatory all my punk rock albums assured me was worse than death. But this became increasingly futile as graduation trudged ever closer. With no plan, no leads, and no income, my fingernails fell victim to incessant, hamster-like nibbling.

Three Fridays later I got home from class to find the red voicemail light blinking on my new cordless phone. It was Kaori from the LUNA Corporation, saying she had some good news for me.

My world fell off its axis. All four limbs turned to silly putty as gravity shoved me down onto the bed, the phone sliding from my fingers and falling to the floor with a plastic thud.

I was going to Japan.


After a long while I regained command of my motor skills and put the phone back in its base. I lurched into the kitchen to pour myself a nourishing pint of Franzia, took a deep breath, and snuck into the den where my roommates were taking a much-needed Nintendo 64 respite from their job search nightmare.

"So... I'm going to Japan."

"What?!"

"Yep, I got the job. I knew I would."

"You're lying. Who the hell would give YOU a job?" I held in a scathing retort. Part of me was dying to rub it in, but I didn't want to tempt the fates. After a stunned silence one of them spoke again.

"Congrats, Matty boy. That's awesome."

"Thanks! Pretty unreal."

"Lucky bastard. So you're gonna teach English?"

"Yep, to little kids."

"Ha! Try not to traumatize any of them."

Senior year had been a rough one. The late-'90s dot-com bubble had burst and unemployment was on the rise. Undergraduate degrees lost their value while student debt soared to amazing new heights. And September 11th didn't exactly help.

Those of us about to enter the workforce were freaking out. Stern voices from all around – family, friends, and professors alike – spewed amateur opinions and plastic pearls of wisdom about life after college, with one central message: everything revolved around a strategic, goal-oriented plan for professional advancement.

These words were echoed by a wretched little Gremlin living inside my head (figuratively speaking), whose favorite hobby was sabotaging my self-esteem with expertly chosen words of pure malevolence. It had been there since around puberty, I suppose, offering up a steady stream of criticism as I navigated my teenage years as an awkward, unattractive loner. It had mellowed out a bit in college, particularly during my semester in Ireland the year before, but was growing louder as I strove to delay the inevitable onset of real life.

what's your plan? live in mom and dad's basement like a bum? get your shit together and find a job! are you trying to let everyone down?

On and on it yapped, relentless and immutable, leaving a smoking crater of anxiety behind my diaphragm.

Then, one Sunday evening just before St. Paddy's Day, an email popped into my inbox with the subject line: "Teach English in Japan." In an autonomic response to anything resembling a marketing email, my hand slid the mouse pointer over the "Delete" icon and my finger rose.

Time stopped. My body froze. Limitless potential realities shook the foundations of my conscious mind, ringing with the promise of destinies yet unmanifest. Fates... converged!

Actually, the truth is that two buddies of mine had recently introduced me to the wonderful world of spicy tuna maki so I was in a pro-Japan mindset at the time. I clicked on the email.

Not for a moment had I ever considered a career in education. My major was Psychology, which I'd declared at the end of sophomore year due to a mild curiosity about why everyone was so screwed up in the head. Between then and now I'd lost interest in the entire discipline, which was probably why I hadn't sent out a single job application. Who wants to be a psychologist, anyway?

But I'd give teaching a shot if it meant the chance to peruse the far side of the globe without having to live out of a backpack or hemorrhage money I didn't have on overpriced hotels and tourist traps. The only pre-requisites were a college degree, which I'd soon have, and an open mind. Check and check. I prided myself on how wide I could pry open my mind in a pinch. And let's face it, I had nothing better to look forward to.

Well, I sure as hell did now. The torment of uncertainty had finally passed, and for now the Gremlin was quiet. As I half-watched the furious Mario Kart battle unfold over the next twenty minutes, the full-body gimp suit of repressed tension that had clung to me the entire year slowly peeled away. My old life had ended while my new one hadn't yet begun, and I floated adrift in a kind of existential limbo. Lucky bastard, indeed.

The official letter arrived right around my birthday at the end of June, after I'd graduated and gone back home to Maryland. It included a pile of information on Japan, a company profile of LUNA, and all the legal drivel on passport and visa requirements. My eyes, however, immediately darted down to the three big checkboxes at the bottom of the page. Box one read: "small town." Box two: "medium-size city" and box three: "large city." All I had to do was pick one and LUNA would do its utmost to place me in a city of my desired size. Simple, right?

I'd just left Beantown and the last thing I wanted was to move to another big city full of bright lights and rush hour traffic and people in a dizzying hurry. My mind was all about the *bushido* code, paper lanterns, and martial arts. How sweet it would be to learn the way of the sword with a company of wandering *ronin* at sunrise every morning, high on a misty mountaintop within sight of the sea!

Yes, my mental image of Japan was both four centuries

out of date and a hundred percent Hollywood stupid. I checked box one.

My plan to kick back that summer went up in a fiery blaze of bureaucracy. For anyone with a mind to pick up and move to a different country, know that the government pretends to take that very, very seriously. There are passports, visas, different *kinds* of visas, proof of travel, proof of employment, entry permits, re-entry permits, medical records, interviews, vaccines, follow-up interviews, background checks, financial statements, and all other manner of written verification that you are a living biological life form and absolutely, positively not a spy. There are no exceptions, loopholes, or shortcuts to any of it.

Mom and Dad were thrilled about the whole thing and flipped the bill for private Japanese lessons, and I was pretty sure I was rocking those. I could count pencils and buy tickets and order drinks like nobody's business. I'd tried nearly every item on the menu at my local sushi dive and couldn't wait to put even weirder things in my body. Heck, I even started drinking green tea.

My new home was called Nagaoka, a town in the north of the country and about twenty miles inland from the Sea of Japan. My first stop, however, was LUNA headquarters in a city called Okayama, a few hours west of Osaka on the southern coast where teacher training took place.

For years I'd looked at air travel with all the fondness of a ruptured hemorrhoid. It's painful, it's degrading, and people shouldn't put up with it. The Japanese, however, are the undisputed heavyweight champions of customer service. They began proving this from the moment I stepped up to the check-in counter.

"Good morning, sir," the agent said as I approached. Her uniform, hair, makeup, and posture were immaculate, her smile and tone so genuine it almost felt like a prank.

"Hi, there!" I replied. I held out my ticket and passport, which she accepted with two hands.

"You are traveling to Osaka today?" There was a splash of British mixed in with her Japanese accent.

"Yes," I nodded as my boarding pass printed.

"Thank you," she said. She asked me all the new TSA security questions as she tagged my bags, then gently placed the boarding pass on the counter in front of me. "Your flight will board at 8:10 a.m. from Gate 22," she explained, circling both numbers on the pass. Then she pointed over my shoulder with an open hand, palm-up and at eye level. "To reach security, walk down the hall and turn left at the doors."

"Got it, thanks!"

"Thank you for choosing ANA! Have a wonderful flight!"

The gate crew met me with the same impeccable manners as the ticketing agent, receiving my boarding pass with two hands, a smile, and a tiny bow. So did the flight attendant who directed me to the far aisle of the cabin and offered me a bottle of water, again with two hands. It was as if I were someone... important? Me, a vile passenger? Important? Preposterous. My cynical Generation X sensibilities refused to believe it.

But it just didn't stop. It didn't stop after I found my seat or at mealtimes, or during the thirteen-hour cruise or after we landed, or upon disembarking through an ocean of smiles and thank-yous. It didn't stop at the newsstand where I bought water or at the Lawson (the Japanese 7-Eleven) by the baggage claim. What the hell was going on? Why was everyone treating each other so well? Did I miss a meeting? Welcome to culture shock. I'd been to two or three other countries before with their little differences, but this was deeper. Courtesy and respect were woven into every interaction. And I wasn't some high-paying client entitled to VIP service. No one was trying to impress me here. This wasn't a fluke or a fad or some fringe hippie bullshit. This was fundamental – a visible behavioral difference resulting from a society-wide belief system I was not brought up on. A warm fuzzy crept into my heart as the contagious power of good manners worked its magic. I could almost *feel* myself softening around the edges.

The sights and sounds of Kansai International Airport were both overwhelming and somehow distant, as if I were watching it all through a window. It was oddly relaxing to be surrounded by a language I didn't speak – I could ignore everyone with no fear of being rude to anyone, which made it easier to drown out the chatter. I heard everything, but didn't overhear anything, if that makes any sense. Bright and noisy as it all was, none of the hustle and bustle around me caught my attention unless I let it. Very bizarre.

I was not ignored in equal measure. People stared at me from every direction. They'd usually lower their eyes if I looked back, with the occasional smile or fit of giggles from wandering packs of teenagers. A few children gaped as if I were the Yeti. It made sense, though – I was a head taller than everyone around and a fresh-off-the-boat *gai-jin* (foreigner).

or maybe it's because you look like you spent the night in a dumpster. and you probably stink.

I ran my fingers through my hair in a feeble attempt to groom myself for this unexpected new audience, but it just made my hands greasy. My kingdom for some wet wipes.

Thankfully, the directions to the designated meeting spot I'd received from LUNA a few weeks prior were idiot-proof. In my current state I couldn't navigate a coloring book. I'd spent a sleepless night on the plane watching Seinfeld on my seatback screen and getting wrecked on something called *chu-hai*, a fizzy, fruity adult beverage of impressive potency – similar to White Claw nowadays, only sweeter and stronger. According to the letter I'd crushed into my back pocket, a representative from LUNA would meet me at 2:00 p.m. to take me to Okayama. I looked at my watch. 8:05 a.m. Ugh. I planted myself on the nearest bench and attempted a nap.

I flopped back to consciousness an hour later. A blonde, round-headed girl about my age sat on the bench across from me, legs crossed and twirling her hair. She was ragged from a trip as long as mine but somehow still wore a smile.

"Hey!" she said brightly as her image came into focus. "Are you waiting to go to LUNA?"

I rubbed my eyes and gulped down a quick, deep breath. "Yeah, you too?"

"Yep, just arrived."

I sat up and introduced myself.

"Nice to meet you," she said. "American?"

"D.C. area," I nodded.

"Ottawa," she replied through a massive yawn. "Fucking hell, if I don't get a shower I may literally murder someone." This is how I met Celine from Canada. We spent a few minutes volleying the usual "strangers in a distant land" chitchat and trading what little information we had on what awaited us. The conversation then drifted to our personal lives.

Celine's demeanor was fascinating to me, her openness stunning. She was both inspirational and intimidating, passing seamlessly between highly-educated student of the world and unapologetic sociopath. In the same minute she'd spit out statistics on West African economic development models and the story of that time she threw a hot dog through the open window of a police cruiser. I fired back with tales of my own deviant teenage behavior and the exchange left us both in stitches.

After another twenty minutes of cracking each other up, we ran out of things to say and gave it a rest. We exchanged the occasional comment on some of the goofier looking passers-by, but for the most part we spent the next two hours sprawled out in a jetlag-ridden torpor, giggling like idiots at the sorry state of ourselves.

Around noon we were met by the next colorful character to join our cabal.

Glenn from Arizona walked into our lives wearing a gray hoodie, a Felix da Housecat T-shirt, and a sleepy grin. Tall and lanky as a basketball player, his half-squinted eyes added to the aura of die-hard raver I sensed right away.

Celine threw him a peace sign as he approached. "Hiya!"

"What's going on, y'all? You here for LUNA?"

I pulled myself to my feet and shook his hand. "Yes, indeedy. I'm D.C. Matt. This troublemaker here is Ottawa Celine."

"Nice!" he beamed. "I love Canadians!"

She shrugged and gave him a wink. "Everybody does."

"I like the shirt, man!" I said as he took a seat next to her.

"Ah, you know Felix?" he replied. Lovers of electronic music in those days shared a sacred bond beyond all understanding. I now had his undivided attention.

"I saw him a while ago in Baltimore," I said. "It was a splendid evening, from the bits and pieces I recall."

"The best shows are always the ones you don't remember in the morning!" he laughed.

Glenn shared in many of the same vices as Celine and I, and was ready to rage the second he stepped off the plane. He had a way of supercharging the states-of-mind of the people around him and we found our second social wind. He'd been placed in Kumagaya, an hour outside of Tokyo, and issued open invitations to crash at his place any time we wanted to visit the capital for a night on the town.

By noon we were starving. I'd sustained myself all morning on honey mustard pretzel chunks and Pocari Sweat (the Japanese Gatorade) and my bloodstream was turning into raw sewage. The three of us didn't feel like lugging our suitcases around the airport anymore, so we searched for the closest thing resembling a restaurant. We found one in no time.

A large, jukebox-like machine stood just beyond the entrance, adorned with dozens of pictures of food, prices, buttons, and a brightly-lit cash slot in the middle. There was no need to read anything or talk to anyone to place an order – an ideal situation for a trio of *gai-jin* newbies like us. The problem was that the pictures were definitely not worth a thousand words; I had no idea what I was looking at. Too hungry to care, I stuffed some money into the machine's mouth and slapped the button for soup concoction #1. It spat out a number and a bunch of change. My two new friends followed suit, and we sat at the nearest booth to reflect on this weird injection of giddy self-consciousness the culture shock had delivered.

Not that things were particularly different, mind you. The real oddity was that so much was so similar – airports were airports, people were people, and people gotta eat. The only difference was in the details. We didn't ride that train of thought any further because our numbers were up in a flash and the guy behind the counter gave us our goods (with a smile, of course). We toasted our first Japanese meal, clinked our bowls together and went to town.

"This is incredible," Celine exhaled after a long silence. Glenn chewed and nodded. I was too transfixed to respond.

The taste summoned to mind the full bounty of the sea with flavors both familiar and strange. The broth was salty, but the various squirt bottles on the table allowed diners to tweak it with a colorful assortment of sweet and spicy overtones. It wasn't "fishy" tasting, but it certainly hinted at it. I picked up a little white disc floating at the top with my chopsticks and bit into it. A sudden crisp. Radish? Chunks of fleshy gray stuff were suspended in the middle, comprising the last layer of content above the mass of yellow noodles at the bottom. There was also a boiled egg cut into halves in there. After a minute I quit trying to figure out what it was and focused on savoring the mystery. By the last slurp I'd redefined the word "ramen" in my vocabulary and vowed never to eat that freeze-dried packaged shit ever again. The three of us moseyed on back to our meeting spot in a contented haze.

When 2:00 p.m. finally rolled around we were joined (right on time) by Emily, one of the recruiters from LUNA. With her arrived two other people in our training group, Toronto Mary and Auckland Chris. All three were pleasant enough, but by then I was neck-deep in a food coma and incapable of speech. We quietly headed towards the platform to catch the next train westbound to Okayama.

# TEACHERS AREN'T BORN

The bullet train snuck up to the platform like a giant steel viper – sleek, silent, and ready to strike. The tinted front window formed a scowling unibrow, with ridges on either side resembling the tightly-clenched jawline of some apex marine predator. It looked downright angry from the outside, pissed off that it maxed out at only 300 kph. The inside was spotless – no trash, no dirt, no stains, and no smell. The rotating seats all pointed forward like a phalanx of well-disciplined foot soldiers.

This was the result of what's known as the "seven-minute miracle." Before each train departs, a highly-trained cleaning crew descends upon the interior. They vacuum, flip the seats, wipe the trays and windows, and go to town on any lingering morsels of uncleanliness with ninja-like efficiency. They sterilize the entire thing in seven minutes flat and vanish without a trace. Check it out on YouTube.

I barely felt the train move as it pulled away from the station. Smooth as butter. It sported wide, comfy seats, heaps of leg room, and ceilings high enough to accommodate passengers even taller than myself. All natural sedatives. Glenn and Celine were already nodding off across the aisle as I sank into my own chair next to the extra-large window. Before I knew it the Japanese countryside was zipping by at remarkable speed. Not an inch of land was unused. Patches of green and yellow farmland stretched to the horizon, accompanied by sporadic plots of land mirroring the blue sky. Several people slogged through these in knee-high boots – rice paddies! The land was joined here and there by farmhouses that were always brown or white, with coffee-colored shingles that reminded me of the *hacienda* styles of Southern California. The cloudy mountains in the distance framed the landscape like a painting.

And the snacks in the vending machines were perfect. Sesame chips, crispy seaweed squares, and a dozen pretzel and cookie creations were on display in the areas between cars. Other machines sold coffee, soda, sports drinks, and several varieties of ice-cold green tea. Since I couldn't read any of the labels I just picked the ones with the tastiest-looking pictures. My belly was most impressed.

Two-and-a-half quiet hours later we arrived at the LUNA training center in Okayama, a block from the station. The two-story complex featured a bunch of small, western-style hotel rooms to accommodate groups of foreign trainees during their time there.

I stepped into mine and crashed immediately. I didn't even shower.

The sounds of people being social nudged me awake again a few hours later. My watch read 8:00 p.m., but my brain and body felt like they'd been awake for days. Or asleep for days. Who could tell? The jetlag had shattered my internal clock. With an agonizing groan I pulled on some pants, grabbed my keycard, and stepped into the hall.

The noise came from the ground floor, which meant they were being *loud.* After a few wrong turns finding the stairs, the drumbeat of chatter led me to the kitchen. Seated around a huge glass table were Glenn and Celine, along with a few new faces I didn't recognize from the airport.

There was Marc from England, Kristina from Chicago, Tara from Canada, and Chantelle from all over the place. They all had the same circles under their eyes. That last one, though, stood out like lightning.

Tall, slender, and caramel-skinned, Chantelle met every definition of drop dead gorgeous. A cocktail of multinational genetic perfection. She spoke with a neutral accent, though a syllable or two carried the tiniest echo of the U.K. With a voice louder and deeper than her appearance belied, she projected pure fearlessness with every word.

"New face!" she boomed as I walked through the door. With two or three strides she'd crossed the room and was holding out her hand. "Hi, I'm Chantelle."

you should have showered.

Celine's voice burst out from the far corner as she waved to me, drowning out everything else. "Hey, Dexter!"

"What's up, Dexter!" Glenn echoed.

I shook Chantelle's hand. "Matt," I said, ignoring the two

clowns in the back.

"He's lying!" Celine cried.

"Yo, Dexter, not cool to lie to someone's face, man."

Chantelle's face broke into a wide, sly smile that could melt a glacier. "Well, I'm sure the truth will come out eventually," she said. Then her grip tightened and she squinted. "You're not a narc, are you?"

"CIA. Special Agent Matt Niner."

"Oh, that's fine then," she said. She winked and let go of my hand, then turned to rejoin the group.

Now I knew where all the noise was coming from. Chantelle and Celine practically yelled at each other from across the table as they threw out ideas on how to ace teacher training the next morning. The two girls were already laying down plans to visit Southeast Asia in the spring, and Chantelle was all in for the first late-night Tokyo thrash fest that was brewing. She was the same kind of crazy as Glenn and Celine. My new cabal had gone from trio to quartet.

The four of us left to explore the neighborhood after the others had gone to bed. Unfortunately, all we found were empty streets, a bunch of houses, and couple of convenience stores. Fortunately, they all sold booze. We loaded up on *chu-hai* and got sloshed back at the training center until well after midnight.


Training began at 7:00 a.m. in the building next door. We gathered in the same type of classroom we'd be using on the job, though this one was spacious enough to accommodate large groups of adults. We took our seats much as we would in a grad school lecture hall, waiting for the professor to walk in and fill our brains with good, healthy smarts. Three of LUNA's training coordinators – Brian, Lisa, and Claire – had arrived early. Brian carried a clipboard and a gigantic cardboard box. He placed it down with great care, almost reverence, upon a small wooden table at the front of the room, giving it an affectionate little pat. Then he turned his attention to us. I thought he was Japanese until he opened his mouth to introduce himself. Seattle.

He launched into an expert presentation on what to expect during the next two weeks – an intensive training on LUNA's trademark English instruction methodology as well as an introduction to life in Japan. He began with a description of the company, including all the who's who and what's what. He didn't spend a lot of time on this, since we would rarely interact with anyone from HQ while we were there. Instead, the first hour focused on the branch schools where each of us would be stationed. Each had a single manager who was the main authority figure. They didn't teach class, but they coordinated all of the sales, scheduling, evaluations, and communications with parents.

"My first manager's name was Kurumi," Lisa put in. "But everyone just called her Manager. I don't think I heard anyone use her real name all year."

"Same with mine," Brian said. "*Manager* is actually the honorific for their position, so it's a bit more respectful than using their name. At least, that's what I always thought. Different people tell me different things."

Claire shrugged. "Just ask them which they prefer, they'll let you know." She then turned to Brian with a sarcastic smile. "Just don't call them *boss lady*."

"I did that once!" he snapped. "One time!"

He shot a glance of playful contempt at Claire and continued as the chuckling subsided. Depending on the size of the school, he said, there could be anywhere from three to more than a dozen Japanese teachers also employed there. The classes they taught weren't total immersion like ours, though. They were more didactic, focusing on things like grammar and sentence structure that didn't require an immersion setting. Most students enrolled in our classes would first take a class with a Japanese teacher; we then provided the environment to apply the things they'd learned.

"The JTs will already know your students, so they're a great resource if you need help with any of them," Lisa said. "And you will."

"JTs are the Japanese Teachers," Claire explained. "You guys are the FTs – Foreign Teachers. You'll hear that thrown around a lot."

As Brian spoke, Lisa and Claire continued to chime in with examples of their own or to reinforce something he'd said. They had plenty of experience to share from inside the classroom, while other times they broke in just to give Brian a hard time. The three of them had obviously developed a tight bond over the course of their time here. It was almost soldierly, like they'd undergone a harrowing journey together and were now giving survival advice to a room full of new boots.

you're among the big dogs now, junior. time to impress.

I adjusted my tie and sat up straighter in my seat.

\* \* \* \* \*

30

*"Ohayo gozaimasu!"* Lisa greeted us on the morning of the fourth day. The resulting silence rang like a bell.

"That means, 'Good morning!' You can expect this to be the first thing you hear every single morning over the course of the next year," she explained. "After a month or two, it'll just fall out of your mouth every time you walk through the door." She said it again slowly, syllable by syllable. "Now you all try!"

*"OHAAUGOZAAMAA!"* the room echoed, followed by titters of laughter.

The trainers nodded approvingly. "Not bad at all, I'd say!" Brian said with a thumbs up.

"Hell, I'm impressed!" Claire agreed. "This is going to be a great group, I can tell already!"

A series of bursting nasal exhalations came from my left as Celine quietly cracked up. It was contagious. Ego went out the window as we butchered a great many useful Japanese terms and expressions that morning. Afterwards, our trainers took turns going over how a typical class unfolded and how to keep the kids engaged despite the fact that they spoke no English and we spoke no Japanese. Since it was total immersion, everything had to be visual. Even if we managed to pick up some Japanese along the way, we were forbidden to use it to teach concepts or even translate words.

They showed us how to drill new vocabulary and explain ideas with body language, walked us through the various textbook titles we'd be using, showed off some clever tricks on how to deal with misbehavior, and, of course, taught us over a dozen songs to sing to the younger kids. Some were classic nursery rhymes from centuries ago, others were

LUNA originals. These were compiled onto CDs that the company printed and stocked in every classroom in every school, so ubiquitous was their utility. We were strongly encouraged to commit them to memory so that we could spontaneously burst into song if circumstances called for it during a lesson.

With three days left, Brian finally addressed the elephant in the room. He walked over to the massive box he'd brought on day one and put his hand on it, tapping it with his fingertips. He then stopped and just looked at it, building the tension for all of us who'd been wondering about it.

"Now this," he said at last, giving the box a little nudge. "This is what the kids live for."

"Are you kidding?" Claire snorted. "This is what *I* live for, dude!"

"It's true," Brian smiled, opening the box and rummaging around inside. "This one is my personal favorite." He then pulled out what appeared to be a white rubber chicken in a tuxedo. He paused for effect, then spun around and threw it with all his might directly at the whiteboard behind him. The nine of us jumped as it impacted with a deafening *thump*, followed by an eruption of giggles as it stuck there.

I leaned over to Celine on my left. "I will do well here," I whispered. She choked back a laugh.

"I'm gonna get me that chicken," Glenn murmured.

"Oh no, that chicken is *mine,*" Chantelle answered back.

"The point I'm trying to make with this little guy," Brian began, peeling Mr. Sticky McChickenpants off the wall and tossing him back into the box, "is that it makes absolutely no difference what you do in terms of your classroom activities.

As long as you're excited about it, the kids will be, too. It can be something as intricate as a game of chess, or as silly as throwing a chicken at the wall. I've actually done both with different students on the same day. But none of that matters. The English is the only thing that matters. All these wonderful games we're about to show you are just the rewards we offer the kids in return for getting the English right."

"Think of them as bribes," Lisa added with a grin.

"Oh, they're totally bribes," said Claire. "If my students know we're playing Jenga at the end of class, they'll be complete angels."

"For me it's dodgeball," Lisa nodded.

The number of super-fun educational activities the company had in its portfolio was staggering – a timeless archive of great ideas brought in over the years by teachers from around the world. The theory behind it all was simple – keep the energy of every lesson at a fever pitch while maintaining dictatorial control over your classroom. Or, as Celine later put it, make the little brats dance on the razor's edge between jubilance and terror.

"Okay, everybody stand up!" Brian spoke with an alarming increase in volume. We rose. "Now take your chairs and line them up against the wall," he said in the same authoritative voice, pointing to the back of the room with both hands as if directing an airplane. We obeyed and were left with a wide-open space in the middle, leaving only the table and the great box at the front.

"This," he pointed to his mouth, "is my classroom voice. It is the voice you will learn to master, it is the voice you will use to command. Your voice is what gives the orders and sets the tone in your class. Think of it as a cross between drill sergeant and game show host. Talking like this must become second nature."

He summoned us to gather around the table at the front, then proceeded to upend the box. Its wondrous contents spilled out before us. My eyes immediately went to the chicken to make a mental note of its whereabouts.

"Okay, then!" Brian began. "Everybody grab a –"

Four sets of arms catapulted forward. Being slightly taller than the rest of us, however, Glenn had the reach. He came in from underneath and snatched up the little clucker a millisecond before my hands could touch it. Chantelle and Celine shot him a murderous look as he held his trophy aloft in triumph. I swore under my breath.

"Looks like we have a winner!" Claire announced.

"I would say so," Brian agreed. "Glenn! You're going first!"

"Oh, nuh-uh," Glenn said, lowering his arms.

"Haha, sucka!" Celine blurted out.

"So the situation is this," Brian said. "You're teaching a class when the wind suddenly blows your lesson plan out the window. All you have is that chicken and some vocabulary cards. You need to come up with an activity, and fast."

Glenn's eyes narrowed as they drifted down and to the left. He froze like that for a full five seconds, and I wondered if the poor guy had blown a fuse. Then he popped into action.

"Okay, so... I'd do what you did before with throwing this guy at the board and making him stick there. Only I'd have the kids draw a card first, and they'd have to spell the word. It's an alphabet game. However many letters there are in the word is how many times they'd have to spin around before throwing. Then I'd draw a bullseye on the board, like this." He walked over to the whiteboard and drew two big concentric circles. On the outside, he wrote *1x*. In the middle ring, *2x*, and in the center he wrote *3x*. "So if the chicken sticks out here by the *1x*, they get however many points equals the number of letters in the word. If it sticks here, they get double that, and if they get it in the bulls-eye they get triple. If they miss completely they get nothing."

"Holy shit," Celine said, loud enough for all to hear.

Chantelle's hand shot up. "I wanna play!" Several others in the group agreed.

"Good, let's try it out!" Brian announced. "Everybody line up!"

It was a gigantic, awful, delightful mess. We spelled, we spun, we reeled, we threw, we laughed our asses off, and we repeated. For a game made up on the spot, it was a blue-ribbon winner.

"Dude, did you just come up with this on the fly?" I asked Glenn after I'd taken my turn and thrown for a solid zero points. I'd drawn *pineapple.*

"Sort of. I did something similar in summer camp a few years ago."

"Genius."

"Thank you, good sir."

We played impromptu games for the rest of the day. Some were duds, others were okay, and a few were a riot. Celine and Chantelle were by far the most competitive, and therefore the most comical of the lot. By lunchtime my stomach ached from the stitches I'd burst laughing at their antics. The whole thing was more fun than I'd ever thought possible in a professional setting.

No two weeks ever went by so fast. Specks of sadness soured the sweet as I bid my cabal *adieu* on the last day of training – we'd all be off in our own cities until we met up again for the winter holiday. Plans for a New Year's Eve invasion of Tokyo were now set, but that was a solid four months down the road. We exchanged many hugs and high fives and scattered to our respective trains.

Chantelle and I shared one as far as Nagoya, a two-hour ride eastward from Okayama. From there I'd continue on to Tokyo and then north to my new home in Nagaoka. We passed the time reliving the hilarity of the past two weeks and hyping each other up for the exciting times ahead. We practiced a bit of Japanese and raided the vending machines between cars. Since we were nervous as hell about starting the job, we both promised unconditional, round-the-clock emotional support once we got our new cell phones.

A half hour into the ride she turned to me and asked if she could ask a serious question. I told her thanks, but marriage just wasn't on my radar. She hit me, then launched into a detailed description of the boyfriend she'd left behind, asking if she was crazy for believing that a) he would wait for her and b) she could change him. As was my wont in those days, I answered with a brutally honest YES to both.

"I just don't think people can change people," I explained, putting as much empathy as I could into my voice. "They have to change themselves."

quit playing the wise man, you sound like an idiot.

"God damn," she sighed. "He just has so much potential. No, I can change him. I totally can." She stared at me for a moment, her crystal brown eyes lined with concern. "You think I'm crazy."

"I don't think you're crazy, I just don't buy it. I mean, if you're so all in for this guy, what are you doing here?" Her teeth clenched and I thought I'd crossed the line, but she eased back into a smile. She took my hand in both of hers and gave it an appreciative little pat. "Good question." Then she groaned. "Ugh, you're such an asshole."

"I know. But I mean well."

"I know, sweetie."

I had a feeling she already knew the answer deep down. Still, if I'd known this was the last time we'd ever speak, I might have answered differently.

Chantelle got off at Nagoya station to catch a train south to her new home in Hamamatsu, turning heads as she went. None of us ever heard from her again.

The buzz of the previous two weeks faded as the *shinkansen* quietly hummed. The scenery became more and more rural as the countryside flew by the window, and tall buildings became scarce. Then they disappeared entirely. Warm rays of quiet solitude washed over me as I approached my new home.

I arrived in Nagaoka on August 31, 2002. I was met at the platform by my Manager, Yuko, an attractive woman in her mid-thirties who was well-spoken and radiated professionalism. Next to her stood the outgoing FT, Erin, a twenty-something American with a distinctively hippie-ish air about her. They greeted me with a genuine courtesy that I gladly returned, but I was too fascinated by my surroundings to make small talk. During the ride to my apartment I gazed out at passers-by like a beagle in a convertible.

"Here we are!" Yuko said as she pulled the car to the side of the road and yanked the hand brake. I stepped out and got my first glance at the gray, anonymous-looking building in which I would reside. We walked into the parking garage and through a set of wide-open glass doors leading to the elevator.

"No security or anything?" I asked.

"Oh no," Erin laughed. "There's no need. Japanese people don't believe in crime. Right, Manager?"

"I don't know about that," my new boss replied, "but this is a very safe part of the town." She pressed the button for the ninth floor.

"That reminds me," I said. "Should I call you Yuko or Manager?"

"Oh, definitely Manager," Erin answered for her. "We've got at least five students named Yuko at the school, so we all just call this one Manager."

"Either one is okay," Manager said.

Erin winced. "Yuko would be so weird. I never think of you as Yuko, you're Manager!"

I followed them to a gray door on the left and Manager handed me a set of keys. Usually, she said, newly-arriving FTs wanted to be left alone for a while after the one-two punch of trans-Pacific travel and intensive teacher training. Right she was. She passed me a hand-drawn map to the school, reminded me to arrive early on Monday, and the two of them graciously bowed out.

I stepped inside.

The click of the front door closing behind me triggered a euphoric rush that hit like a tidal wave. My bags fell out of my hands. I ran out to the balcony, beheld the nation that lay before me and threw my hands in the air, king-of-the-world Titanic style.

I made it. I'd done what none of my mild-mannered ilk had ever dared do, crossing land and sea beyond the distant horizon to stand fearless in a foreign land, ready to rock, ready to rage, ready to conquer.

On Monday I had a looming encounter with an ill-tempered bitch named Reality.

# CHILDREN GOOD AND EVIL

Like most students, four-year-old Hiro entered the school accompanied by his mother and wearing the expression of a child both cheerful and highly curious. Cute little monkey – what a great student to begin my teaching career with! He puttered around in the lobby while Mommy chatted with Manager, who reminded her that, beginning today, Hiro's private lessons would be administered by the new guy. After throwing me a smile and a quick bow, Mommy turned to Hiro to give him the good news.

She must have badly miscommunicated the situation, instead informing her son that he was to be immediately fed to a three-headed mutant Tyrannosaur from Neptune. His head whipped around as I beamed and waved hello. Our eyes met. His jaw dropped.

The neighborhood dogs lifted their heads in alarm as a high-pitched shriek echoed across the countryside. My ears rang as Hiro flung himself into the arms of his mother, crippled by a terror he'd never known. Manager stifled a laugh and disappeared into the staff room.

Nothing had prepared me for this. An unruly child was one thing, but one bawling like the damned? Was I expected to be both teacher and exorcist? The smile never left Mommy's face as she muttered sugar-coating nothings to her dear frightened child. He wailed even louder. Not knowing what else to do I grabbed the nearest toy – a bag full of little plastic fruits. I reached in and pulled them out one-by-one, feigning bedazzlement at their sudden appearance and pretend-devouring them without mercy.

"Look, Hiro! What's this?" Mommy prompted in broken English. "Ooh, apples! Yum, yum, yum!" Bless her heart, she was trying. The boy didn't notice.

Sweat erupted from every orifice as my core temperature rose to a boil, my undershirt gripping my torso like a wet dish rag. My mind went blank. Were those two weeks of teacher training just a hallucination? Oh, crap, we're still in the lobby, aren't we? Everyone in the school must be hearing this ungodly racket.

Manager re-appeared behind the front desk wearing an apologetic grimace and motioned to my classroom with a little shooing gesture.

this is pathetic. you're humiliating yourself.

My heart thumped like a hammer as I withdrew to the sanctuary of my small classroom, glancing out the window as the volume of Hiro's torment sank by a few precious decibels. My vital signs stabilized with a deep draft of life-giving oxygen. I blinked hard, dropped the bag, and stretched out my arms to reaffirm my alpha status in this small territory, then landed a crisp double-slap on both cheeks to steel myself. The panic subsided just enough during those brief moments of calm to take inventory of the weapons that might aid me in my fight against this malevolent toddler that sought my undoing.

It was all useless – songs, vocabulary cards, games, and other learning materials designed for calm, submissive children eager to learn. Half the drawers and cabinets were filled with junk Erin had left behind, the purpose of which I couldn't fathom. The silver bullet eluded me.

Fuck it. The kid was here for an English lesson, and an English lesson he must receive. I just had to grind my teeth and go through the motions.

"Just get him into the classroom," I whispered into the ether.

Suddenly my eyes landed on something I was saving for the end of the class – a kind of grand finale I'd crafted that morning that was meant to bring Hiro's theoretical joy to soaring heights. I'd been optimistic when the day began.

Cut a square cardboard box along one edge and then straight across the diagonals on either side, and you create a hinge on the opposite edge on which the whole thing will open and close. A bit of imagination and it looks like a big, chomping mouth. With some construction paper, a few markers and a bit of patience, even the least artistic hands can create a somewhat convincing hungry barnyard animal. Erin had left behind a cow. I threw it out and made a dragon.

I grabbed it and scattered the fruits across the floor of my empty classroom. Then I started to sing.

"I like to eat… I like to eat… I like to eat… APPLES, APPLES, APPLES!" I tossed the first fruit into the air and caught it in the box. Mr. Dragon's jaws snapped shut around the succulent Red Delicious. "Yum, yum, yum!" I sang louder. "I like to eat… I like to eat… I like to eat… BANANAS, BANANAS, BANANAS!" The yellow Chiquita disappeared into the fire breather's gullet. "Yum, yum, yum!" Louder still. "I like to eat… I like to eat… I like to eat… MANGOS, MANGOS, MANGOS!" It was actually a pear, but I didn't give a shit. Hiro was still in the lobby. Plus, I was kind of enjoying myself, taken by a giddiness that only a spontaneous eruption into song can deliver.

"GRAPES, GRAPES, GRAPES!

PINEAPPLES, PINEAPPLES, PINEAPPLES!

MELONS, MELONS, MELONS!"

By the seventh or eighth verse I was fresh out of fruit. Whatever. Mr. Dragon retched hard and vomited everything right back to the floor, and I took it again from the top with even greater verve and vigor.

"I like to eat…" I stole a quick look at the doorway. Hiro stood quietly transfixed by the spectacle, his mother holding his hand behind him. "I like to eat…" I spun and kicked an orange to his feet with Messi-like precision. "I like to eat… ORANGES, ORANGES, ORANGES!"

And with that, I plopped down on the floor next to him. Mr. Dragon's mouth hung open while my body sat frozen like a statue, my face turned away over my shoulder. A tense moment passed and I wondered if the doorway would be empty when I turned around again.

The gentle *plunk* of plastic hitting cardboard echoed like

the choirs of angels, and the day was mine. "Thank you, Hiro!" the dragon roared as I jumped to my feet to continue the song.

Small victories.

The boy only pulled himself together for a handful of brief interactions over the next half hour, and only when he was attached to Mommy. She twice tried to sneak out of the room while I had his attention, but she was twice caught in the act and berated for her treachery. I had no problem with her staying; she was instrumental in thwarting Hiro's repeated escape attempts. Plus, part of me actually sympathized with the little hellion. I was an absolute goliath next to him and the first male teacher the school had ever had.

With the clock ticking, I whipped open the book to the day's lesson and sat down on the floor, hoping that Hiro would be a sport and join me. He stood up without a sound, walked over to Mommy, and collapsed in her lap. It was like his battery went critical and he put himself in standby mode. Mommy stood up, Hiro in arms, and thanked me kindly. She then walked out of the room a full seven minutes before the scheduled end of the class.

I sat there like a trauma victim, drenched in sweat and reeking of failure. The sound of happy students enjoying classes with competent teachers permeated the walls around me.

Manager stuck her head through the door. "Are you okay?"

"Yes!" I lied, standing up again. My next class started in ten minutes.

"We all have problems with Hiro, so don't feel too bad,"

she said. "I think you just scared him because you're so big."
"Next week will be much better," I replied through a desperate grin. It wasn't as much a statement as a prayer.

My second class consisted of two sisters – Yuko, ten, and Hitomi, seven. I could smell the fear as they stepped into the classroom and took their seats.

I greeted them enthusiastically, the immediacy of this next class pushing the previous one right out of mind. My smile was returned, but only by the elder. Hitomi's gaze never left her big sister.

I stuck to my lesson plan like a map to water in the Sahara. After introducing the vocabulary cards, there was an activity where the kids would shout out the new words (or sentences) three times fast, then do something silly like spin in a circle, bounce a ball, or do a little dance. Whoever did it fastest would win the card, which counted as a point. It was just a way to get them out of their seats (this lesson was at an actual table) so the class wasn't forty-five minutes of motionless sloth. Most of these "3x" activities ended in a tie, and there was only one way to resolve a tie.

"This is my *nose*! This is my *nose*! This is my *nose*!" the girls shouted in a single voice before flying around the table and landing in each other's seats with a crash. It was a photo finish.

"Too close to call!" I announced. "Rock, paper, scissors!" Little did I know the fury I was about to unleash.

Yuko and Hitomi leapt to their feet, reached back as if to throw a knockout punch, and heaved themselves forward in one swooping motion, screaming "ROCK, PAPER,

SCISSORS!" at the top of their lungs. I nearly fell out of my chair.

Rock, paper, scissors is a sanctified art among the children of Japan, and one they've mastered beyond compare. Far more ubiquitous than in the West, it serves as the go-to conflict resolution tool for every imaginable schoolyard dispute. The results are unassailable and victory is honored absolutely. Hitomi won that round with scissors – the boldest of all rock, paper, scissors tactics – and was beaming. Yuko giggled at the wide-eyed expression I wore.

The class progressed with no shortage of awkward silences as the three of us stumbled over our own nerves. The sisters sat like statues for the most part, which came in handy when I had to stop everything to check where I was in my lesson plan. This happened a lot. We all breathed a collective sigh of relief when our time was up, and the two of them left in a hurry. It was either a successful failure or a failed success. I couldn't tell.

Next on the docket was Yuko and Hitomi's mother, Sayaka. It was common for a parent to have a lesson immediately after their children, while the kids had a second class at the same time with one of the Japanese teachers. A parent might want to learn English to help them at their job, or they might have a trip to Europe or the States coming up. Others wanted to learn just for the sake of learning. Sayaka was one of them. There was a book series for adults on hand at the school, but she preferred organic conversations about whatever topic was interesting at the time. Plus, she'd survived the minimum eight years of English required by the Japanese public school system and was already at a pretty high level. We talked about family, traveling, food, life in the U.S., and, of course, her kids. She was soft-spoken and mellow to the core. It was a welcome respite in the middle of a tumultuous first day.

My energy reserves were critically low by the time my last student arrived. Kana was her name, and it was clear when she collapsed into her chair that every subsequent moment would be a struggle to keep her eyes open after a long day of school, sports, and whatever else her parents made her do before she walked through my door.

I did my utmost to fire the afterburners so at least one of us wouldn't be catatonic the entire time, but lethargy is contagious.

"How are you?" was the first thing I asked her.

"Tired."

I had no delusions about the semi-demonic nature of fifteen-year-old girls. I'd been to high school. Imagine my surprise when, even with zero desire to be there, Kana was pretty respectful. Her English was also damn good for her age. From time to time I picked up on a barely-audible grunt of exasperation, particularly when I made her stand up and move around, but never the slightest hint of non-compliance.

Halfway through the class I looked at my lesson plan. *Textbook exercise, p. 22-24.* I pulled out my book.

"Ah, noooo…" Kana groaned, hanging her head.

"What's wrong?" I asked.

"I don't have my book. I never use it. It's stupid."

I silently agreed. I'd flipped through the book that morning and it did strike me as a tad moronic. Today's lesson was supposed to focus on the different rooms of the house and the furniture therein. How useful is that in a survival sense?

"Did you use the textbook with Erin?" I asked.

"No."

Good enough for me. "Okay, then. What should we talk about?" I tossed the book over my shoulder so hard that it slammed into the whiteboard behind me, causing a bunch of smiley magnets to rain down onto the floor. Kana let out the first laugh of the hour and the tension in the room broke.

"Music," she said.

"Really? What kind of music do you like?" I asked, reminded at once of the enormous influence of music on the life of a teenager.

"Pearl Jam," she answered immediately.

Not in my own Top 20, but I could work with it. "What's your favorite Pearl Jam song?" I asked.

"Buraku."

I shook my head. "BLLL-ack."

"Buraku."

"One more time. BLLL–" I pointed to my mouth, where I bit the tip of my tongue to make the *L* sound. "–LLLack." It was a notoriously difficult sound to make; the letter didn't even exist in the Japanese alphabet.

She stuck her tongue way out and chomped down like she was about to bite it off. "BLLL-aku!"

Every syllable in Japanese ended with a vowel sound, so consonant endings were also tricky. This was why nearly everyone called me "Matto sensei." English words ending in -*ck* were nearly always spoken with a -*ku* ending instead.

"Blll-a-CK!" I said again, pounding my fist on the table with the final -*ck*.

"BLLL-A-CK!" she repeated, slamming her own fist much harder.

"Black."

"Black."

"Excellent!" I cried, holding my hand up for a high-five. Kana smacked it hard and was glowing. "Now let's try *Yellow Ledbetter*."

"Nooo!"

The door shut behind Kana at 8:00 p.m. and my first day of teaching was over. My legs were ready to buckle – never in my life had I felt so utterly drained.

that was a fucking disaster.

Manager and a couple other JTs were watching me intently, as if half-expecting me to collapse into a fetal position and sob like an infant. They burst into a high-pitched, "Yaaay!" and a round of applause.

"You survived!" Manager declared.

"Yeah," was all I could say. My mind had short circuited. A vacuum hummed from some far corner of the school as the rest of the staff began the nightly ritual of cleaning up the place. I offered to help, but Manager was having none of it.

"Go home and rest," she insisted. "You must be hungry."

she's already looking for your replacement.

I took in a quiet moment before heading out for the night. An eerie serenity lingered in my now empty classroom – it was like looking at a crime scene. The horrors to unfold inside these four walls would test me again and again, my endurance and fortitude pushed to their very limits. My real training had begun. This was my world for the next 364 days. Or until they fired me.

While most of my students behaved just fine, there were always a few who sapped my will to live and left me a burnt-out corpse at the end of class. These little demons in human skin took the names Akina, Shun, Yuri, and Satan's little helper, five-year-old Misaki. They were the ones who did *not* want to be there and didn't give a dusty fuck if I knew it or not. All I could do was put on a happy face and just grind it out, week after miserable week. My only hope was that they would feed off my false positivity when it went into overdrive, but Lord knows it didn't always work. It even backfired on occasion, especially with Misaki, who took any kindness on my part as a green light for mischief. She even flipped me the bird once or twice. Five years old.

I had a few gems as well, I won't deny it. There was Sumika the genius and Akihito the goofball. There was Takuma, who reminded me of myself with his twelve-year-old Nintendo geekery. And, of course, there was shy little Yukiho with the ponytails that practically reached the floor.

But my favorite by far was Hinako, the human equivalent of a strawberry cupcake with rainbow sprinkles. This four-year-old cherub brightened up the entire school every time she walked through the door. She loved to be there, and it showed. She arrived every Wednesday morning five minutes late, wearing a spaced-out look as Mommy helped her out of the coat and pink boots she always wore. Then a smile would leap to her face as she bolted full speed to the end of the hall and back again. Cries of *Hinako-chan!* came from the JTs as she flew by their classrooms. Adding a *-chan* after a girl's name showed extra affection.

Her cuteness was stupefying. She had chubby round cheeks and a button nose, which is all you really need when you're four. She was a bit nervous when our first class began, but that faded fast.

Right away she spotted Mr. Dragon and her eyes widened. She walked over to the bookcase, picked him up and began muttering to him in Japanese. I could only assume she was introducing herself.

"Hello, Dragon!" I said, waving like a crazy person.

"Hello, Dragon!" she repeated. The smile grew on her face – a wide, toothy one that took up half her head. She smiled at pretty much everything.

"Do you want to give Mr. Dragon some food?" I asked.

"Yes," she responded, handing him to me. I launched into the same spiel I'd done with Hiro, this time to a captivated audience. Every time Hinako dropped a fruit into Mr. Dragon's mouth she giggled and did a little pirouette. She listened attentively when we reviewed the vocabulary cards and spoke with her index finger extended like she was defending her dissertation. She danced around at every song and gave high-fives with gusto. By the end of our forty-five minutes together I thought my skull would collapse under the weight of sheer adorableness.

"Say goodbye to Matto sensei," Mommy said on their way out. Hinako ran back and threw her arms around my leg, looking up at me with another massive smile.

"Bye, Matto sensei!"

My skull collapsed.

# THE SHRINE IN THE FOREST

It was a lovely little apartment – modern, clean, and impressive in how it optimized the limited space available. Flawless hardwood flooring covered the main corridor that stretched from end to end. To the left of the front door was a shoe rack, while to the right a crossbar was mounted in a recessed area for hanging coats and such. Next to this a door opened into a large utility room. Inside was a washer/dryer to the right and a shelf for ironing and folding clothes, which I never did. On the far wall was a white plastic vanity for making myself pretty in the morning, far larger than my limited cosmetic accessories demanded. To the left was a folding door that opened up into a kind of self-contained plastic closet, with a standing shower on one side and a bathtub on the other.

A kitchen (if you could call it that) was built into the wall of the main hallway. It was nothing more than a sink, two cabinets, a microwave, and a single gas burner. To the right of this was a slender refrigerator/freezer with a Mr. Coffee on top that looked long overdue for retirement.

Opposite the fridge was a tiny little room with a light blue toilet. To the edge of the seat was attached something that resembled one of the control panels on the starship *Enterprise*, chuck-full of mysterious little buttons with Chinese characters written on them. I bared my rump and sat down, curiosity getting the better of me. A few of the buttons had little icons suggesting some manner of hydraulic utility. Imagine my surprise when I started pushing them at random and discovered a state-of-the-art bidet with every imaginable bell and whistle.

The living area lay at the end of the main hall. The balcony was accessed by a sliding glass door on the far wall, which was flanked by a waist-high bookcase on the left and a TV stand on the right. On top of this sat a 13" idiot box that got only local channels. Useless. A small but powerful A/C unit loomed above with a remote control attached to the wall beneath it. Against the wall to the left sat a black, fake leather loveseat with a foam interior, light enough to pick up but firm enough to support even *my* hefty backside. In the corner to the right a traditional Japanese futon lay neatly folded on the floor in front of a closet. Mattresses, frames, and box springs were a rare thing in Japan. I eyed the futon with skepticism at first, but it was as comfortable as any bed.

Within those 600 square feet I was lord and master of all the earth, the lone survivor of some mass extinction event. I could be as neat or as slovenly as I pleased. I never had to step over some else's clothes or wonder who mucked up the sink. I could positively ID every item in the fridge and no one else ever ate the last of anything. Hell, I could walk around butt naked if the mood took me. And at any time I could step out onto the balcony, see the mountains, and behold the wide world at my feet. It was an apt visual for the freedom I'd found. Bonding with my first sovereign living space was pure joy those first weeks abroad.

Unfortunately, novelty fades.

The loneliness crept in as the weather cooled down. My little rural town suffered from a chronic lack of goings-on. I had no cable and no internet at home, and watching the same two-dozen movies on my laptop was getting really old. This was before the days of Wi-Fi, iPhones, and WhatsApp. I was so fried from teaching nine hours a day I had no mental capacity to even learn Japanese. Worse still, I didn't have any energy to be sociable, so I hadn't made any friends. On occasion I'd go out with a few of the JTs for dinner or to hit the bars, but this was the limit of my social circle in Nagaoka. If Glenn and Celine weren't answering my texts for whatever reason, I'd spend whole evenings out on the balcony just listening to music by myself. Even on the weekends nearly all my free time was spent alone, either at home or out exploring the town on my bike.

Oh, and there was no Thanksgiving in Japan, and I'd be working on Christmas. Eve *and* Day.

I rode along the bank of the river that bisected Nagaoka on one of the last semi-warm mornings of 2002, determined that I would finally cross that humungous bridge to see what

I could see. I'd passed by it countless times before, but something had always held me back. It wasn't much to look at and there didn't appear to be anything terribly interesting on the other side. Still, it was uncharted territory and something about my hesitation to tackle it had been gnawing at me. I pulled the headphones out of my ears and started across.

It was a pleasant traverse. The bridge was flat, smooth, and relatively light on traffic, only a dozen or so cars interrupting an otherwise heavy silence. Footpaths on either side offered easy crossing for bikers and pedestrians. Scattered patches of farmland stretched out from the near bank for a hundred yards or so before the river itself made an appearance, suggesting that in ages past the water level had been quite a bit higher. Perhaps a dam had been built upriver somewhere. Halfway across, my ears perked up at the sound of flowing water and the land yielded to a wide, slow-moving torrent. I stopped at the center of the bridge and dismounted, standing my bike against the rail and leaning over the edge to listen for a while. I was always a sucker for that sound.

A renewed bounce in my step coaxed me into taking the rest of the bridge at top speed. On the far side, a horizon of unmarked buildings vanished into green hills far beyond, where the sky had begun to darken with the threat of unwelcome precipitation. At the end of the bridge the road broke off into four directions at a traffic light. None of them stood out as any more intriguing than the next, so I kept going straight for simplicity's sake. More turns just meant more ways to get lost on the way back.

I passed little houses, convenience stores, more little

houses, a school, and even a construction site or two. This side of town was no more thrilling than the other. "To hell with it," I thought. "Let's find those hills." Another half hour went by and the low battery alarm on my legs started buzzing. I stopped as the road ended at a T-intersection. To the left stood yet another row of houses, while off to the right the road made another sharp turn and headed back in the direction I just came from. I hung my head and blew a raspberry as the first raindrops tapped on my scalp. Then I looked straight ahead. A large grassy expanse lay where the road would have kept on going. I couldn't believe I'd missed it.

The road *did* keep going. It had just changed. The asphalt was replaced by an ancient-looking, cobblestone path that continued on for another three hundred yards at least. This was flanked by narrower strips of brown earth, ground down like the tracks beneath some monstrous wagon. About halfway to the end, the path was met by a series of huge stone obelisks on either side that reminded me of giant chess pieces, each of them different in size and design and serving a purpose I couldn't begin to guess. The way forward faded from sight just before disappearing into a dense tree line – a huge, impenetrable wall of green like the border of some arboreal fantasy realm. A tiny dome of pitch black at its base suggested a threshold of some sort. The path led right to it.

What was this place? A park? A cemetery? The familial estate of some wealthy aristocrat? Most importantly, was I allowed inside? Was this a public space, or would I be shot dead for trespassing by some random… what was the Japanese equivalent of a gun-toting redneck?

I wasn't about to set foot unwelcome on holy ground, if

that's what this was. On the other hand, nothing about it *felt* unwelcoming. There were no signs, no gates, and no guards. I sensed no evil spirits and smelled no stench of the undead. No dark magic of any kind, in fact, despite my imagination running amok with images of the elvish road through Mirkwood. I parked my bike at the edge of the street and stepped onto the path, instantly pleased with myself for doing so.

I walked as though the eyes of the world were upon me, comporting myself with dignity even though there wasn't a soul to be seen. When I reached the obelisks, their true enormity stopped me in my tracks; each was at least seven feet tall and looked like they'd stop a wrecking ball. Hollow compartments at their pinnacles suggested they'd once been great stone lanterns, illuminating the path for nighttime visitors who'd wandered this way centuries ago.

The way ahead became more visible as I approached the tree line. The light beneath the canopy was dim, but enough to reveal the path creeping into the woods for several yards before turning left and vanishing again.

Off to the right a massive amphitheater had been dug into the ground, its circular rings of earthen stadium seating covered by patches of grassy undergrowth. At its center was a large pavilion that looked like a newer addition, beneath which was a flat, circular space that bore the blackened scars of countless bonfires. Next to it stood an enormous flat stone as tall as I was. Mounted on a much smaller base stone, its edges were adorned with a palate of moss and lichen that reflected every imaginable shade of green. Its face was covered by three columns of etched calligraphy, the middle one sporting by far the largest font size. Had I been able to read *hiragana,* the native Japanese alphabet, it might have offered some clue as to what I was looking at. As it was, I simply marveled at its handsome aesthetic and wondered how many years it had stood watch over the place. I turned back to the path and stood at the threshold of the trees. Thunder rumbled in the distant sky. My hand went to the hilt of my imaginary sword, half-expecting a swarm of ninja stars to come buzzing at me from every direction. I mustered my fortitude and plunged into the accursed forest.

The path continued much as it had for the past quarter mile, albeit now surrounded by trees. I followed the leftward turn and the grass behind me disappeared from view as if a door had shut. Nagaoka vanished. I was now countless miles from civilization, a wanderer lost in time and space.

From deep in my mind a single thought of purest serenity emerged. Or did it come with the breeze? With the clear voice of a Sage it spoke – calm, fearless, and wise, and unconditionally on my side.

*This is what we've been looking for.*

It was euphoric. For one shining moment, everything clicked right into place. Had I really just thought something so wonderful? Giggling stupidly, I made a slow, 360-degree turn to drink in the full splendor of the forest before continuing on.

I came to a bridge. Its base was made from the same kind of stone that covered the path, but carved into longer, narrower slabs. It might have spanned running water at some point. But that purpose had long vanished, giving way to a dry riverbed overrun with olive green foliage. Though it was only about twelve feet across, there was a kind of magic to it. There's something special about crossing a bridge. The stairs came into view as I reached the far end. Up and up they went, dozens of them, high enough to obscure whatever lay beyond. A pair of great seated lions stood watch on large, square pedestals on either side of the summit. Carved in the eastern mythical style, these grim-looking sentinels had the facial features of both man and beast, contorted into grotesque, threatening smiles. They were made of some kind of metal, bronze perhaps, that reflected an unnatural, reddish hue that contrasted with the abundant greens and grays of earth and stone all around. I stood beneath one and met its eyes. The expression it wore was unmistakable – "Touch me, and I swear to Christ I will jump up from this platform and murder you in ways you can't imagine." I knocked gently on its rump and heard a dull *clang*. Definitely metal. Fortune smiled as it did not to come to life and disembowel me that day.

A second set of stairs took me up again before passing under a lofty, Japanese-style *torii* gate that may have once been painted gold. It looked like wood, which was confirmed by the familiar sound my knuckles drew from it. Such traditional gates were associated with Shintoism, the indigenous religion that predominated before the arrival of Buddhism. To pass through one meant you'd left the material world behind and were now on sacred ground. A ballet of pins and needles danced on my skin as I stepped under it, my shoulders relaxing for no earthly reason. I froze and listened to the silence that had deepened with every step.

My eyes drifted shut for a while.

The sound of water tapped my eardrums and I was

brought back to earth. I followed the path around one more turn to the left and it finally met its end. The last twenty yards were flanked by six more stone lions, three on each side and set on pedestals about four feet high. The first two had their heads turned and were looking right at me, offering a touch of genuine creepiness that threw me back into memories of those demon gargoyles in *Ghostbusters* that scared the hell out of me as a kid. Off to the right was a small pavilion, unadorned and modern-looking. The sliding glass window at its front reminded me of a ticket counter, or perhaps a refreshment stand, above which was a large white sign covered in black Japanese writing. Straight ahead lay a larger, far more impressive building.

The central structure of the complex solved the mystery of what I'd stumbled onto – undoubtedly an old Shinto shrine. Its frame was capped by an enormous rooftop that rose and fell into several peaks and troughs, drab but beautiful. It was hard to believe the slender wooden columns upon which it rested could support is bulk. Paper lamps, ropes, and scattered pieces of cloth hung over the entrance, while various signs had been erected at the base of the five stairs leading up to it. These must have been announcements for upcoming events of some sort; one was printed on a horrid bright pink canvas. Yuck.

The hardwood floor groaned in welcome as I stepped inside, but there was no one to hear it. The wide, empty space in the middle was covered by a spotless *tatami* (woven straw) mat, which reminded me to kick off my shoes. Ahead along the far wall was an open display of statues, cloth banners, altars, vases, and other symbolic pieces of art and sculpture I couldn't identify. Several candles were lit and I could smell incense burning. A large, black canvas was mounted above, adorned with flowing calligraphy all in white. The walls to the left and right were mostly bare, though dozens of small metal lanterns hung from crossbeams from end to end. The only sounds were the distant chirping of birds and the gentle, chaotic rhythm of a bamboo wind chime somewhere outside. The thunder had stopped.

I sat down on the floor to take it all in, the buoyant force of utter tranquility guiding my hands across the coarse fabric of the *tatami*. It wasn't until I felt the lunchtime rumble in my belly that I decided to be off. But I'd be back. How could I stay away? Finding this place was a straight-up miracle, as if a higher power had guided me to a hidden patch of Eden lost in time and perfectly preserved. And it was all mine.

After one final look around, I started down the path back to the 21$^{st}$ century.

In separate excursions I discovered the only movie theater in town, a fairly decent gym, and a fully-stocked music shop. The owner let me play on the guitars (even though I sucked at it) and I ended up buying one after my second visit. On the ride home that day I came across another prize – a *kaiten* (conveyor belt) sushi joint three blocks from my building. I jumped off my bike and stepped inside. I was greeted by an enthusiastic *Irashai!* (Welcome!) and curious stares from the local patrons as I took a seat on the nearest stool and put down the Fender. The parade of fine sushi danced in circles before me like an exquisite culinary ballet. I reached out and grabbed a plate of shrimp. My eyes then spotted the plate of *maguro* tuna on the far side, slowly making its way towards me like a minnow to the gator's jaws. I stared with murderous intent as it rounded the corner to my left and into striking distance. In a flash it was gone, snatched up by the gentleman sitting two stools down. Thwarted. Denied. Robbed of my prize. I stared at the thieving son of a bitch for several incredulous seconds, but my gaze was not returned. None of the other customers noted this appalling act of larceny as the thief munched away on the tasty red morsel that was rightfully mine. I turned back in defeat to the shrimp I'd seized a minute prior. A pitiful crumb scavenged from the dregs.

*"Hai, dozo!"* (Here you go!) came a commanding voice. I looked up to the center of the belt, amazed I hadn't seen the chef standing there the entire time. In his hands was a plate of *maguro* being thrust in my direction with an unfamiliar mix of both force and courtesy. I hesitated for a split second, wondering what the hell was going on. Then it hit me – he'd spotted my reaction to what just happened and made a fresh one just for me.

My head fell into a bow as I accepted with two hands. *"Arigato gozaimasu!"* (Thank you!) I cried far too loudly, drawing one or two more stares. He smiled and gave a quick nod before returning to his work.

The tuna was such a deep red I thought my eyes were bleeding. I delicately separated fish from rice and submerged it in the shallow pool of soy sauce and wasabi I'd blended with my chopsticks. Placing it back together again I picked the whole thing up, raising it to eye level to examine it more closely. It was exquisite to look at, while its gentle aquatic scent filled my head with images of deep-sea diving off Cape Cod. I placed it in my mouth and bit down. A symphony of fishy flavors built to a crescendo as I chewed, slowly and deliberately, before the wasabi said hello and it all went down the hatch. Only then did I breathe again.

I made a full visual sweep of the restaurant, nodding approvingly as if I'd built the place with my own two hands. The fates had spoken – this was my new dive.

On my way out, the sweet old lady behind the counter handed me a little green card with two holes punched in it. She pointed and spoke a couple of quick sentences, in a friendly (but vain) attempt to explain what it was for. I smiled and nodded, feigning understanding. It looked like the cards I used to get at Subway to mark how many sandwiches I'd eaten in my quest for the coveted free tenth. But what happened when I reached the final hole? Did I get a prize? A free dessert? My picture on the wall? An irresistible new imperative suddenly lay before me. I must unravel this mystery. Honor demanded it.

*"Arigato gozaimasu!"* I said.

"You're welcome!" she replied, giggling.

On my seventh or eighth visit one Sunday afternoon, the place was buzzing with patrons and there were two chefs on duty instead of the one. I planted myself on a seat at the far end of the counter, where the conveyor belt disappeared back through the wall and into the kitchen on the other side. It was a poor choice; all the good stuff got snatched up before it circled around to me. There was plenty of sushi to be had, but most of it looked like it had been sitting on the belt for some time and had dried out. Common sense told me to avoid those.

I was just about to get up and find a new seat when someone cried out.

*"Toro!"*

My head whipped around like a dog spotting a squirrel. I knew that word. *Toro* was tuna belly – the softest, fattiest, most succulent part of the whole damn fish.

*"Hai,"* the chef responded and immediately went to work. In less than a minute he handed off a plate of freshly-made tuna belly to the lucky man who'd called for it.

Wait a minute... could *I* do that? Just shout out what I wanted and they'd make it for me? That wasn't condescending as hell? Two other people answered for me in the minutes that followed, bellowing orders at random as if it were the most natural thing in the world. A giddy sensation ascended from my midsection to my face and my palms went clammy. My mind went into overdrive.

*I'm gonna do it... I'm gonna do it... here goes!*

please don't.

*"Toro!"* I cried.

look at the idiot, everyone.

A resounding *"Hai!"* answered back.

After a few self-conscious moments I leaned forward to watch the act of creation now unfolding before me. The chef worked with blinding speed, assembling with the skill of a master craftsman. A long, thin knife of folded steel cut through fish like a light saber, then was wiped clean and returned to its holster in a single deft move. Rice and wasabi were rolled and packed to perfection by fingers that could have easily belonged to a concert pianist. The knife flashed one last time as he lifted the two completed pieces on the flat edge and placed them onto the plate next to him.

"*Toro,*" he said, handing it to me.

I flashed my teeth and nodded. "*Arigato gozaimasu!*"

"*Hai.*"

The plate was orange. I'd never had an orange plate – what was this new devilry? They'd been stacked up behind the counter next to all the others, of course, but I'd only ever eaten anything from a red or a yellow. This was a custom order, though, and a higher-end item than any I'd sampled so far.

Now, on previous visits I'd always just stood up when I was ready to leave, throwing the chef a thumbs up and acting like I was looking for my wallet. The cashier would then come over and count the empty plates next to me, jot some figures on the bill and hand it to me with a number circled at the bottom. I paid without hesitation, confident that there was no chicanery at work. But now a momentous discovery – the colors were the prices! Reds and yellows were a hundred and two hundred yen, respectively. Oranges were five hundred, blues were seven hundred, and whites were a thousand. What a moron I was for not piecing it together sooner.

My attention returned to the *toro* before me. Lighter in color and less rigid than the *maguro*, it glistened with the promise of latent deliciousness. I'd only tried it once before back home, where a single piece would run anywhere from twelve to twenty-five bucks. Here I was looking at twin pieces for about five. I proceeded with my ritualistic soy sauce lather and paused for dramatic effect before it disappeared into my salivating gullet. My neck went limp and my head dropped. I barely had to chew; my jaws simply tightened and the whole thing dissolved in my mouth. It was less fishy and oilier than I'd remembered, and far more flavorful.

I looked at the second piece. "Five bucks," it whispered, shameless and seductive. I tore the fish off the rice and popped it into my mouth, *sashimi* style. A thousand pinball machines sprang to life on my tongue.

Sushi would never be the same again. I'd been spoiled rotten.

# BETTER LIVING

I texted often with Glenn and Celine as we formulated our New Year's Eve Tokyo rage-a-thon. The plan was to meet up at Glenn's place in Kumagaya two days prior and use it as a base of operations, ninety minutes out from the capital. As the holiday approached, however, the plan deflated. Chantelle was missing in action, while Celine had fallen for a local and decided to nix Tokyo in favor of true romance. Humbug.

"Nah, don't even worry about it, man," Glenn reassured me when I called him with the bad news the night before. "We'll still have hella fun. It's kinda nice to not have to worry about the girls, anyway." Something in his voice told me he'd expected this all along.

"Right, then!" I said, jumping onto his wavelength. "What's good in Kumagaya?"

"Lots. My buddy Taka is spinning at Club 19 here tomorrow night, so that'll be fun. It's my go-to spot, always good times. My other buddy Riley is coming over on Saturday to hook us up with whatever we need for our brains."

Twelve hours later I stepped off the platform at Kumagaya station. Glenn stood outside chatting with a Japanese dude who was all smiles and wearing a New York Yankees hat. He greeted me like a long-lost cousin, pulling me into a crushing hug and slapping me on the back.

"So, you work with Glenn over at LUNA?" Taka asked as we started walking.

"Yep, but I'm up in Nagaoka."

"Where's that?"

"Up in the Niigata prefecture."

"Oh yeah, of course. I've been up that way a few times to go skiing. It's really nice up there."

"It's nice, there's just not much to do."

"Yeah, it's out in the country a little bit so it can be boring. Especially if you don't have a car."

"Riley let me drive his car once," Glenn chimed in. "It was like the scariest thing I've ever done." The Japanese drove on the left, which was backwards and terrifying to Americans like us.

"So, Taka, where are you from?" I asked.

"Uhh, I'm from here, man."

I waited for the punchline. "Seriously?"

"Yeah, man."

"He is!" Glenn said. Taka gave a little shrug.

"Holy cow, your English is *perfect!*" I said, amazed. "I thought you were from Malibu or something."

"No, it's not perfect," he laughed.

Glenn clapped him on the shoulder. "I told you, man! You sound like pureblood California!"

We walked for about five blocks (I assumed in the direction of Glenn's apartment) before stopping outside a kind of miniature strip mall.

"I'm hungry," Glenn said suddenly, turning to me. "Have you been to a McDonalds yet?"

I looked up and spotted the Golden Arches dead ahead. "I have not, sir."

"Good for you," Taka said with an approving nod.

"Yeah, but you should go at least once," Glenn said as we stopped at the entrance. He held the door open for us. "I'm buying!"

"Okay, you guys go crazy," Taka replied. He was clearly not feeling a Happy Meal just then. "I'll meet up with you again tonight."

"No doubt," Glenn answered. The two of then exchanged an exploding fist bump and he was off.


*"Irashaimase!"* boomed from behind the counter as we stepped inside. Glenn bounded across the floor in zero seconds flat and was already ordering when I walked up. He threw down a ¥10,000 note and pocketed the change without counting it. Two paper bags appeared on a familiar brown tray. Glenn grabbed it and spun around, heading for the stairs. "Let's do this!"

The second floor was empty, so we planted ourselves in a table by the window overlooking the street. Glenn pulled out three sandwiches from the first bag and handed them to me. The second was filled to the brim with French fries. "So I got you two of my favorites and a standard cheeseburger as a backup."

"A wise strategy," I replied. "What should I expect, here?"

"The unexpected," he laughed, chomping down on his first victim.

I unraveled the white and orange paper to reveal a croquette with pickles and mayo on a bun with no seeds. I bit into it and my face contorted – not with disgust, mind you, only bewilderment. "Shrimp?" I mumbled as my jaw relaxed again.

Glenn nodded, watching me intently. "Wait for it…"

A spark ignited in the back of my throat. "Wasabi in the McShrimp?!"

"Yup."

"Madness."

I ate more attentively once the surprise had worn off. It was relatively fresh tasting, had a nice bit of crisp and just the right amount of mayo. It wasn't too oily, nor did it feel like a rock in my stomach afterwards. By the last bite it had won me over.

Two sandwiches remained. I'd planned to have the cheeseburger as a palate cleanser, but my hand chose that moment to be insubordinate and grabbed the weird one instead. The paper was an ungodly shade of pink that did nothing to suggest anything edible. I pulled it off and examined the thing underneath. It vaguely reminded me of the old school McRib they used to serve back in the day, only without the signature oblong shape. The smell suggested something sweet… barbecue sauce? I took a bite and winced as a syrupy eruption devastated my mouth. My taste buds cried out in anguish as my tongue reluctantly came up to help move things along. I reached out for my drink and crushed an empty paper cup I'd neglected to fill.

Glenn's voice came from beyond a parallel universe of grossness that had enveloped my being. "You want me to grab you a soda or something?"

I waved a finger in the negative and came back to my senses, ripping open the cheeseburger and stuffing as much of it as I could into my half-full mouth. The beefy goodness washed over my teeth like a healing tonic, while tiny onions neutralized the horrid sweetness that pervaded. Two flavors battled for supremacy like Hector and Achilles before the gates of Troy. Neither was victorious, but called for a tentative cease fire after suffering grievous losses on both sides.

"That was pretty bad," I uttered at last. "What was it?"

"Teriyaki burger," Glenn chuckled.

I smushed the whole thing back into its wrapping and dropped it in the bag. "Let's never speak of this again."


Glenn had gone to great lengths to transform his apartment into a lair of maximum coziness, and he'd done it well. Makeshift wall-to-wall carpeting had been improvised from an eclectic yet tasteful layering of rugs and fuzzy blankets. All about the floor were oversized pillows to sit on, and there was no shortage of goofy-looking stuffed animals. Nearly every inch of wall was covered in posters, photos of musicians, weird bits of art, old event flyers, and exotic-looking fabrics, so there were interesting things to look at all around. In the far corner was a wooden cabinet, on top of which sat a spiraling glass candelabra next to a little fish tank housing a half-dozen tetras and one of those little black goldfish with the humungous eyes. A desk fan next to his computer gently circulated a trace of incense in the air.

My gaze landed on a round, blue plastic toy. *"Doraemon!"* I gasped. I recognized the time traveling robot kitten from a hundred different students' backpacks and notebook covers. I snatched him up and held him aloft.

"Yep, my students are all mental about that guy," Glenn laughed. "You ever watch the show?"

"Nope, I only know him by reputation."

"It's really weird. Taka made me watch it once when we were baked. Freaked me out a bit."

I tossed it back on the couch. "You have only yourself to blame for that one."

The sun had just set when a man walked through the front door with barely a knock. He was shorter than I was, but with a darker complexion and a build that said he was no stranger to the gym. His button-down Hawaiian shirt revealed a large gold chain around his neck, and white Oakley sunglasses covered half his smiling face despite the lack of sun. He sported green cargo shorts and flip flops in defiance of the freezing air outside. Dazzling flecks of light leapt from several large gold rings between his knuckles. But what really stood out were the enormous mocha-colored dreadlocks that exploded out of his head and fell to his waist. In his left hand were two plastic grocery bags nearly bursting at the seams.

"Smells nice in here!" he said in a slight Middle Eastern accent before turning to me. "You're Matt, yes?"

"Hey, how's it going?" I replied, extending my hand.

under no circumstances are you to trust this man.

He shook it with the grip of a titan. "Riley. Nice you meet you, my friend." He put the two bags on the table, then fell onto one of the many pillows with a sigh. Before I could blink three cans of *chu-hai* appeared and he was tossing me one. "Cheers!" he said brightly, pushing the sunglasses to his head and cracking his open.

He and Glenn chatted for a while, mostly about local people and places I was clueless about. Riley was very interested in the details of Glenn's love life, but appeared unsatisfied with the answers he'd pried out of my friend. He turned to me.

"So, Matt, what about you? You found yourself a girlfriend yet?"

"Nope, still solo." A response we young men are rarely proud of.

"You like girls, though, yes?"

"Oh, yeah. I am *constantly* thinking with my dong."

"Damn, you too?" Glenn said.

"Well, you let me know," Riley smiled. "My wife knows a lot of Japanese women who would love to marry a tall, handsome *gai-jin*!"

That statement lingered for a moment before detonating. He was serious. An astonishing reality revealed itself for the very first time – with college behind me, I now inhabited a world of *married people*. Until the end of my days I would walk among them, puzzling over their cryptic behavior and non-linear methods of communication.

"I can't get married," I replied, quoting one of my favorite films. "I'm a thirty-year-old boy."

He chuckled for a second, then stopped short and threw me an incredulous look. "Wait, you're thirty?!"

"Twenty-two."

He slapped his knee as if I'd said the funniest thing ever. "I like this guy, man," he muttered in Glenn's direction.

Riley was out the door again in less than an hour. However, it wasn't before he'd handed Glenn two tiny plastic bags half-full of brown powder. He'd picked them up on his last trip to Osaka, where dubious things could be purchased from street vendors if you knew where to look. Drug laws in Japan were far less comprehensive than those in the U.S., so there was a whole gray area about what was and wasn't strictly legal. Rumor had it that for years you could buy magic mushrooms from the vending machines. The substance now in our possession was called AMT – some processed witch's brew conjured up decades ago for well-intended but highly abusable purposes. It was one of the milder narcotic options for the more risk-averse party peoples of the world.

We spent that evening bar hopping some of Glenn's favorite watering holes before heading to Club 19 around midnight. Taka was already in the DJ booth when we arrived. It was pitch dark, but surprisingly smoke-free and not too loud. There were only a few people dancing, but they were doing it well. For the next few hours we popped on and off the floor, jumping around like idiots whenever the music crescendoed. Taka's genre of choice was described as "progressive house," known for long stretches of time during which the music would slowly build to a series of thunderous, track-defining peaks.

We waited out the more mellow intervals at the bar, shouting ideas about how to best close out the year tomorrow night. Glenn had heard wonderful things about a club called Liquid Room and was eager to investigate.

I just couldn't wait to see Tokyo.


"Shibuya, that's the stop we want," Glenn called to me over the heads of our fellow commuters on the afternoon of December 31, 2002. We'd taken the regional train south from Kumagaya before transferring to the subway somewhere northwest of Tokyo. In stark contrast to the luxury of the bullet train, we were now bricks in a wall of people aboard an unimpressive public transit unit that could have belonged to any city on earth. The map over the doors was unreadable, so we kept our ears on the intercom for *Shibuya* and *tsugi,* which meant "next."

At each stop people boarded the train like an offensive rush during an AFC playoff game. It was hard to believe. How could such a famously courteous people abandon their manners in such a thuggish fashion? Is this what big city life did to people? The driver wasn't slamming the doors on us like they did back home, so the mad haste was inexplicable. But then I saw it… these folks weren't pushing each other; they were *being pushed.* As the doors opened and people squeezed by each other to disembark, a trio of official-looking chaps took positions behind the crowd waiting to board on the platform. They sported black suits, white gloves, and hats that made them look like commercial pilots. The vice of human meat tightened again as the fresh victims lurched aboard. The car reached its capacity and all movement ground to halt, leaving a half-dozen folks still standing just beyond the doors. The chaps placed their palms on their backs and began pushing with all their might. A groan emerged from the crowd like a note on the world's most pitiful accordion.

Faces contorted all around as the fresh air mutated into the festering aroma of a mosh pit. I watched in disbelief – not so much that we were being mushed together like canned tuna, but that everyone willingly let it happen. Try this on the D.C. metro and fists would fly. Not here. This was how it was done and everyone knew it. What's more, the savagery was actually *working!* Crude as it was, the chaps managed to cram every last person aboard and get the doors shut in less than a minute. The train didn't skip a beat and we were off again.

*"Tsugi no… Shibuya…"* the comm system croaked fifteen minutes later. Next stop Shibuya! The cold air rushed in as the doors slid open and we waddled our way to freedom. The station exited out to a star-shaped intersection of monstrous size, in the heart of a pulsating commercial district that instantly reminded me of Times Square. Or was it Vegas? Tall buildings extended off into the distance in every direction. Countless store fronts adorned in colorful neon signs illuminated the block with a pale lavender light, bright enough to make the street glow. Walls of pedestrians loomed on every corner ready to charge, while cars, trucks, taxis, and buses of every shape and design glided swiftly but quietly by in five directions. Then it all stopped. *All* of it. The red lights shone and the intersection froze in time. Then came the exodus.

A mass of humanity heaved itself into the street like a stampede of wildebeest. Glenn and I stepped onto the flat, asphalt square as the swarm of city-goers approached from the opposite side. A cry of fury exploded in my head as I became William Wallace at Falkirk, storming the battlefield to engage my oppressors in a bloody melee. My eyes widened as the two armies met. The stampede was suddenly a hornets' nest – folks buzzing about in mad, darting motions as they tried their best not to slam into each other. I slowed my pace enough to look around – it felt like crowd-surfing at a heavy metal concert, only my feet hadn't left the ground. The moment was short, however, as a faceless blur bumped me back to normal speed. Now I was Han Solo, piloting the Millennium Falcon through the treacherous asteroid field in *Episode V.*

The skies cleared and we stepped onto the sidewalk once again. Glenn was chuckling; he'd gotten a kick out of that, too. I turned to watch the traffic burst back into action and was overwhelmed by the urge to do something silly.

"Let's cross again!"

Glenn nodded and gave me a thumbs up, turning to face the street. "When it turns, we charge!" I bounced on my toes in anticipation.

The lights turned red once more and two crazy *gai-jin* bolted forward, only to stop dead in the middle of the intersection. We threw our hands in the air as the human waves rolled by, then stood alone like monoliths in an empty street. Three seconds before traffic resumed we dashed back to the sidewalk, immensely pleased with ourselves despite the many strange looks thrown our way.

"That was totally worth it," Glenn said.

We popped into a music shop or two, but for the most part we just walked the streets and took in the sights. There was some time to kill before it reached a respectable clubbing hour. Plus, it was cold (late December cold, in fact) so we looked for a place to hunker down and pre-game before the main event. By some miracle there was an Irish pub across the street from Liquid Room. It wasn't nearly as packed as you might expect for New Year's Eve and we actually scored a table in the back. About two hours and three pints later Glenn passed me one of the bags of AMT.

I twirled it in my fingers, inspecting it closely over my half-empty Black and Tan. It looked like dirt.

"Should we do this now?" I asked.

"Yeah, it's probably a good time," Glenn said before upending the wee plastic square into his mouth. "This one comes on slow."

The apprehension of introducing a toxic substance into the bloodstream made my heart flutter, as if warning against impending danger. It was good to know the ol' survival instincts were still working. I took a deep breath, poured the dust into my hand, and licked my palm clean. It tasted like it looked.

you're going to die.

"A toast!" Glenn blurted out in an uncharacteristically loud voice. He raised his vodka tonic high above his head, beaming. "To drugs!"

"Hear, hear!" I answered, draining my glass.

"Now let's find us some beats and make love to the music!"

Liquid Room was decked out in full form and color for the occasion. Glittery "Happy New Year" signs sparkled on every wall. Countless party streamers hung from the ceiling like brightly colored stalactites, giving the place a distinctly subterranean feel. A huge, golden "2002" was projected onto the far wall beneath a monstrous disco ball. The bar area to the left was chock full of people. Most of them were Japanese, but there was a solid number of *gai-jin* as well. The bartenders all wore party hats, bead necklaces, and oversized plastic sunglasses. This whole scene was of little interest to us, and we turned our attention to the source of the booming soundtrack. The intensity surged with each step down the terraced lounge area towards the dance floor. Like any good EDM venue, the lines were clearly demarcated between those who were there to socialize and those who were there for the music.

As if to personally welcome us, the DJ unleashed "Da Funk" by Daft Punk just as we reached the edge of the floor. An old girlfriend had gotten me addicted to this tune years before and it remained one of my all-time favorites. I shut my eyes and surrendered to it. The music commanded and my body obeyed, and before long there was nothing separating soul and sound. Every now and then it dipped into something I didn't particularly like and I'd pop back to reality, the Gremlin offering up its usual bile about how I couldn't dance to save my life. God knows it was true. Fortunately, He invented tobacco for such times. I bit cotton and conjured fire, drinking in the healing fumes and giving thanks unto Saint Joe, the patron saint of camels, tar, and emphysema.

Out of nowhere the DJ stopped everything with a

backwards record spin, screeching the world to a deafening halt. The lights went out and an impossible silence gripped the club for three full seconds. Then the hammer fell. A single, dissonant note of enormous power erupted from all around, trembling my very bones. It changed to a higher pitch and all fell silent again. Glenn appeared from somewhere behind me, grabbing me by the shoulders and jumping up and down in a fury.

"This is Moby!" he screamed. "This is 'The Ultimate Fuck Song!'"

He hadn't gotten that last word out before the beat dropped again. A pulse of bass shook my rib cage as the kick drum struck, while that first dissonant note came and went in a repeating loop. A woman's voice shrieked *"Oh, yeah!"* to meet it, providing the only vocals. The track was equal parts glorious and terrifying, like an exploding volcano. I'd never heard anything like it.

The wall behind the DJ booth suddenly burst into a blinding white light. Projected in huge silver writing was the number 20, which spun out of frame as the number 19 spun in. Then 18... 17... 16... The crowd cheered as the countdown began. The floor was packed with people now, all on their feet, all wearing expressions of unfettered joy. The place went off like a supernova as the number hit zero and the world entered 2003. My beautiful, blessed human family. I loved every one of them.

Glenn and I raged at that same frenetic level for the next three hours. We danced and roamed and smoked and became fast friends with random strangers, swapping war stories with fellow *gai-jin* and giving English tutorials to a few giggling locals. When the break dancers had come and gone around 4:00 a.m. and we could boogie no more, we drifted towards the exit.

We stepped out into the cold and were gripped by a silent reverence. It had begun to snow. Tranquility enveloped us like a blanket, as if we'd just emerged from the wardrobe into Narnia. The chill stabbed like a dirk through my sweat-drenched clothes, but the wound was cauterized by a narcotic numbness from head to toe. I chuckled as steam rose from Glenn's head, giving him the appearance of a recently blown-out matchstick. He grabbed his hat and yanked it down over his skull. I did the same and we started walking.

"I need orange juice."

"Totally. Lawson?"

"Lawson."

I reached into my pocket and pulled out a phone number written on a scrap of torn up cigarette box. Kylie. I laughed out loud, not from a sense of achievement but that someone had actually brought a pen to a nightclub. I showed it to Glenn. "Any ideas?"

"Yeah, I saw you making out with some chick earlier." He clapped me on the back. "You don't remember?"

"Mmm, not so much. Australian, maybe? Was she cute?"

"Couldn't tell."

"Nuts."

There was no shortage of 24-hour convenience stores in the big city, but Lawson was the most reliable. It consistently stocked a healthy assortment of salty snack treats and high fructose corn syrup. We relished the warmth of the store before headed back out again with a renewed supply of

Vitamin C. The streets were completely empty. I imagined half the world passed out after too much champagne, snoring on someone else's kitchen floor and in for a truly rude awakening later this morning. We walked in silence, shielding our faces from the wind.

Glenn stopped. I turned and saw him a few steps behind me, staring ahead with a quizzical look and chucking stupidly.

"Ohhh, lordy," he mumbled. "We didn't think this through, did we?"

"Huh?" I followed his gaze. "Oh." Shibuya station lay directly ahead, dark, devoid of people, and gated up like a fortress. Words failed me. We shared a long, contemplative silence, rooted on the spot.

"You know," I mused. "Normally a little Gremlin in my head would be cussing me out right now for not planning better, talking all kinds of shit. But now, nothing." I pointed to my temple. "Quiet – like the dark side of the moon."

"Yup," Glenn nodded. "AMT does the trick."

"Indeed. My mind is bent but my head is clear."

"Right?"

"It'd be nice to get your brain like this without the chemicals. Just like, bam!" I snapped my fingers. "Chill like this all the time… just going through life… like…" The rest of the sentence died in my mouth.

Glenn clapped his hands and rubbed them together hard and fast to warm them up. "Whatever, I still feel good! What time you got?"

"Four oh twelve in the *mañana.*"

"I think the station opens at seven, so that's not bad. We should keep the blood moving, though. Let's walk and talk."

"Lead on, Pocahontas!"

We checked the station doors just to be sure. Definitely closed. We headed around the back and came across a huge, gated vent in the street that opened down into the subway tube far below. A blast of warm air rushed up to meet us as we stepped onto it.

"Holy crap, this is amazing!" I laughed. "It's like a hot shower!"

"I know, right?" Glenn said. "There's another one!" We rounded the corner into an narrow alley. A normal person might avoid dark urban spaces like this in the middle of the night, but Japan's streets were famously safe. The wind from this gate was as warm as the last, but it was quieter and didn't blow quite as hard. It was also a welcome dry spot on the otherwise snowy asphalt, so we plopped down on our butts.

Glenn lit up two cancer sticks and handed me one. "It's like the Buddhist monks, man."

"Say what?"

"What you were saying before. They go through life all Zen and stuff with no drugs at all. I think that's part of the Shaolin Kung Fu training, like mind over matter so they can do all that crazy ninja stuff. I saw some of that when I was in Myanmar. Visited the temples."

"Burma. Nice."

"Yeah, it was wild. Groups of monks just sitting around getting their Zen on. It was like… you could tell they were in a zone. You couldn't distract them no matter what you did. I didn't try, but you know. Guys were like rocks. And they're not on drugs or anything, man. They just DO it."

"Nike, son."

"Ha!"

We sat there in our little oasis of warmth, talking at length about this and that while running out the clock. The passage of time was a drifting fog. I leaned forward to rest my head on my knees.

A door slammed shut somewhere and I was pulled back to the waking world. My eyes cracked open as a pitiful groan emerged from the back of my throat, a festering desert of citrus and ash. A thin carpet of snow had accumulated on my shoulders as dawn arrived, illuminating the alley in all its disposable glory. Dumpsters, wooden crates, and huge cardboard boxes had watched over us while we dozed. My knees locked as I tried to stand up, a bolt of electric cold shooting up my abdomen and into my aching back. It was like trying to bend a popsicle without breaking it. Pins and needles shot through my Achilles tendons as my feet took my weight, while the sound of traffic hummed from beyond the building behind us. I pulled out a frozen hand and looked at my phone. 8:25 a.m.

I brushed the snow off myself and looked down at Glenn, curled up in the same position I'd been in. His eyes were wide open.

"You awake?" I croaked through the sandpaper in my larynx.

"Sure am," he replied, springing to his feet. "I didn't really sleep, I was just chillin'. Didn't want to wake you. Ready to roll?"

"Yes."

I'd officially slept on the street. Mom and Dad would be so proud.

# BURIED

The snow hit the second week of January, dumping two feet of powder on Nagaoka in less than 48 hours. With the daily commute like a trek through the Siberian tundra and half the students arriving soaked and grumpy, a noticeable gloom descended on the school. There was bad news from home as well – a good friend's dad had died and I couldn't possibly fly back in time for the funeral. On top of that, the entire D.C. area was being terrorized by a couple of lunatics shooting people dead with a sniper rifle from inside the trunk of a car.

All these lovely updates came via email, which became less and less accessible as the weather worsened. The only internet connection I had was on the computers at the community center a few blocks from the school, and each trip there was a battle with the elements I was loathe to wage.

Not that it mattered much those days – the invasion of Iraq was all anyone was talking about. I'd reach out to friends back home with detailed accounts of this wacky new life I was living, wanting nothing more than to BS with them for a while and feel a bit less forgotten. Instead, my inbox drowned in politically charged replies with various iterations of *"Fuck Bush!"* or *"Fuck Rumsfeld!"* instead of the light-hearted banter I was starving for. I'd been unplugged from the mass media machine for so long that the whole mess in the Levant was barely real anyway. No one was interested in how I was holding up way out here.

The warm solitude I'd basked in when I first arrived mutated into cold isolation and it was a daily struggle to stay positive. "What the hell am I doing here?" became a frequent question to myself when my students got on my nerves. Their English wasn't improving much, either. It was silly to think it would in the few short months I'd been teaching, I suppose, but I couldn't shake the notion I was letting them down. Was it possible I wasn't the master *sensei* I thought I was?

The answer came when Manager handed me my schedule for the new year. Nearly half my students weren't on it. What gives? I wasn't that bad, was I? Most of the missing names came as no surprise – they'd been coerced into my classroom only by parental tyranny – but one or two of my favorites had gone, too. The loss of Sumika the genius stung hard.

My eyes raced across the page for Hinako's name, a sudden breath of panic filling my lungs – still there, right where it should be. Meltdown averted.

"Don't worry too much," Manager said, reading my

bewildered expression. "Many students leave after the first-year enrollment discount."

"Still, this seems like a lot," I said.

She nodded. "I was surprised. It's more than usual. I think it was a really big change to have a man for a teacher. You have some new ones, though!"

"That's true," I replied, trying to sound cheered up. The sense of loss festering in my stomach had no rational explanation. What did I care if a few of the little weasels were someone else's headache now?

"Someone from Okayama will call you tonight to talk about it," she added.

My phone rang just as I was getting home. Claire's voice was on the other end. We exchanged the usual business-casual chit-chat before getting to the point.

"I heard you're losing some of your students this year."

"Are the bosses mad?" I asked.

She hesitated. "No. But we always reach out to our FTs when it happens, especially if it's more than we typically see. It can be really upsetting sometimes."

"Yeah," I said, and I meant it. "I'm surprised I feel so crappy about it."

She followed me out of formality. "You grow attached to them, right? Even the ones you think you don't like. My second year I had this little monster, Rai, who made my life a living hell. He was the absolute worst, and I burst into tears when he didn't renew. The teacher-student relationship is weird like that. There's nothing else like it."

Claire assured me things would get better if I just hung in there, that winter was always a rough time, and that the folks at Okayama were always there if I needed help with anything, work-related or otherwise. I thanked her, hung up, and was a million miles away again.

I stepped out onto the balcony into the freezing cold. The moonlight was amplified a thousandfold by the snow covering every surface, giving the terrain a dim, ethereal glow. I coughed at the first intake of frigid air and longed for summer. Then I texted Celine.

> I JUST LOST LIKE HALF MY STUDENTS
>> SO?
> DUNNO. FEELS SHITTY.
>> THAT SUCKS.
>> YOU LOSE ANY?
> NOPE, THEY GAVE ME NINE MORE.
>> THAT SUCKS.
>> HAHA

I stepped back inside and fell onto the couch, my incompetence confirmed. I dropped the phone and tried to think of something to do. Nothing. My music library was played out and I had no internet to download anything new. I'd re-read every book and watched the life out of every DVD I had. I fiddled with the guitar a bit, but since I only knew power chords it offered about ten minutes of distraction. I even thought about cleaning the apartment, but it already shone. Up until then I was still glowing from having a place all to my own, and quiet Friday nights were a genuine pleasure.

That was gone now. My Shangri-la had become Cell Bock D and the walls were creeping in. I sat there staring at my laptop.

you know, you can always quit. you gave it a shot and realized this life isn't for you. nothing wrong with that.

It couldn't hurt to cultivate a few options. Just in case, right? Put a few irons in the fire? Unfortunately, there was only one place to begin. My teeth ground in the back of my jaw as I reached for the mouse and slowly navigated to My Documents.

Few activities in life had ever brought me such a singular misery as updating my resume. It was its own breed of awful. But there the wretched file was, an unwelcome speck of bile on my hard drive. I hung my head and double-clicked the icon. My spirit whimpered as MS Word opened up.

no one will blame you for throwing in the towel. besides, it's not like...

Without warning, the forest shrine came flying from my memory into my mind's eye, along with a familiar voice.

*No. This is exactly where we're supposed to be.*

I could almost *feel* the discord in my brain. Never before had the Gremlin been stopped dead in its tracks — the little bastard had a way with words and an intensity to match. Plus, it knew my weaknesses and how to prod them. Then, out of nowhere, the Sage had struck it mute with a message of power and hope.

But wait, they were both *me*, right? So, what the hell? Was this how people went crazy? Nah, I was pretty sure I still had all my marbles. I shut down my computer and sat there contemplating, with an odd sense of gratitude that the better part of me had scored a point.

Then I snapped out of it, suddenly incensed that I'd had such a horrible thought to begin with. Throw in the towel? Just give up? Forget about the last six months and run back home to momma with my tail between my legs? To hell with that. Quitting would be catastrophic, unforgivable. The last thing I wanted was to look back years from now and lament a terrible choice made in a moment of weakness, a golden opportunity botched in what could very well be the only life I'd get. I couldn't leave Japan in failure just to end up right back where I'd started. I needed all this to be a win. Besides, my career options hadn't changed much since college, so what else was I going to do?

I stood up and swore to myself I'd power through until my contract was up in August. Then I could conclude my time here, successfully rather than prematurely. An honorable discharge of sorts. That would be my victory.

But I was still angry. A line had been crossed.

The Gremlin had always been annoying, but now it was attempting something truly insidious. *How dare it* try to get me to walk out on Japan. It wanted to convince me I was ugly? *Fine.* That no one liked my jokes? *Great.* That I'd been wasting my time, money, and effort on this and that? *Super.* But try to push me into making one of the worst decisions of my life just because things weren't going to plan, and we're at a whole new level. Those were the actions of an enemy. An enemy in my own goddamn mind.

No, not *in* my mind. The Gremlin wasn't some foreign object or parasitic organism invading from without, it only felt that way. The enemy *was* my mind. A bit harsh, perhaps, but I needed to regard it as nothing less when it acted against my interests. And that's exactly what it was doing. If I let it keep trying to convince me to leave Japan, sooner or later it would work. Or maybe not. Either way, it was a risk I wasn't willing to take. The stakes were too high.

And so the bell rang on the mental title bout of the century. Strength in one corner and weakness in the other. The Sage in the blue shorts, the Gremlin in the red. And the latter must lose.

Silence the Gremlin.

But where to begin? What the hell was I even talking about, here? How does a guy change the way his own mind works?

Meditate or something?

# SAVED

Bruce Lee had a famous one-inch punch. It popped into my mind one cold Sunday morning while I was still in bed, searching my memory for anything on the subject of mental discipline. The legend was he'd floored men twice his size with a single punch thrown from the distance of his fingers. It was like he could hyper-focus the totality of his physical, mental, and spiritual energy (whatever that was) and channel it directly through his fist in weaponized form. However he did it, the result was devastating. No one could withstand it; he'd tapped into something immensely powerful.

Without realizing it, I'd clenched my fist.

"What the hell," I thought. "Gotta start somewhere." I pulled myself up to a seated position and concentrated hard on moving all my energy into the fist of my right hand, Bruce Lee style. Nothing happened, of course, but I didn't care. I had no other ideas. I kept at it.

Before long, my mind started to wander into those wretched places where the Gremlin lurked. I couldn't stop second-guessing the whole endeavor.

don't just sit here, go do something useful! learn japanese, socialize, exercise, get laid, or any of the thousand things you could be doing instead!

Perhaps I could have tapped my energy reserves to get out there and be productive. Was I wasting my time just sitting here? The feeling was hard to shake. Fortunately, the Sage had a different opinion.

*We're in Japan! Every moment here is time well spent. Take a deep breath, ignore the Gremlin, and just be you.*

Back and forth it went. Whenever the Gremlin attacked, I clenched my fist tighter and let the Sage counterstrike with that miraculous, cosmic reality – I was in *Japan!* Nothing the Gremlin could throw at me could touch that. It washed through me with every breath as I practiced driving all the activity in my brain down into my Bruce Lee fist.

The sheer volume of thoughts, images, questions, and memories flying around in my mind was astonishing. Pure chaos gone unchecked for twenty-two years. Clearing it out was like throwing on the hi-speed wipers on the freeway during a torrent – the moments of clarity were incredibly brief. I constantly had to start over. All those pictures of people meditating in movies, magazines, and drug commercials made it look effortless, as if all I had to do was open my heart and the healing energy of the celestial tides would carry me out to sea. Wrong. Meditation is an active exercise that requires time, patience, and commitment. Fortunately, my life circumstances let me muster all three. Just barely.

I soon discovered there was no way I could separate the happy thoughts from the bad ones. It was all just muck, and that's where the Gremlin lived. It all had to go fist-ward.

I wonder what Glenn and Celine are doing? Fist. What happened to Chantelle? Fist! That girl on the train today was smoking hot. Fist, dammit! I'm hungry. Snack on fist! Is it bedtime? I can sleep when I'm fist! Slouching? Okay, that one's true... sit up straight, young man. But then fist! Fist! *Fist!*

Before long I had fingernail marks in my palms – the only physical evidence of the melee inside my brain.

At first I never meditated for more than twenty minutes at a time – the battle for thoughtlessness wore me out too quickly. Images flew into my mind from every direction, and all I could do was try to drive them out as soon as I noticed them. It was exhausting.

But the days and weeks went by and the stretches of time I was able to keep the muck fist-bound slowly got longer. Seconds turned into minutes. Minutes turned into more minutes. The longer the session, the more potent the medicine.

It was a revelation. For years the Gremlin had prowled around my head with limitless toxic energy, unchained and without mercy. Now I knew it could be subdued, quietly incarcerated in the ball of my first. It was my first glimmer of control over something I never thought could *be* controlled.

I practiced making the "mind-fist separation" every night before bed throughout the rest of winter. On the good days I'd stand up and putter around my apartment, just to see if I could stay thoughtless while actually *doing* stuff. I tried washing dishes, picking up clothes, re-arranging books, and writing in my journal while trying to keep my mind empty. It never worked. The world is a distracting place no matter how small, and even the most banal tasks set my mind adrift. I still had a long way to go.

In March I headed back to Okayama for "follow-up training," a week-long retreat for all the FTs to share ideas, vent frustrations, and hone our teaching skills. For me it was an excuse to reunite with the cabal and find out how much trouble we could pack into seven days. Glenn and Celine were already cracking each other up when I arrived at the training center that evening. The common room was full of people I didn't recognize, but my two accomplices were easy to spot. Glenn sprung to his feet.

"What's up, boyyy?!" he boomed from across the room. Four or five other FTs raised their heads in alarm as he strode in my direction.

"Not much, amigo, how you been? Still hungover from Liquid Room?"

"For real. I've had Moby on the brain ever since! You coming back to Kuma for round two?"

"Just waiting for the next vacation," I replied as we walked over to where Celine was sitting.

"Hey, loser!" she greeted me, smiling as ever. She patted the seat next to her.

I sat with a look of deep offense. "Loser, what? How dare you, madam?!"

"Ha, ha. So you guys slept on the street in Tokyo, eh?"

"Briefly. What's it to ya?"

She shook her head in disdain. "I am SO glad I didn't go with you. Neither of you would have made it out of there alive."

"Oh, you would've hated it, girl," Glenn said to her. "Nothing but boom boom techno and party people."

"Yuck."

"Okay, enough of that," I declared, eager for news. "How's life with both of y'all? Gimme all that sweet, sweet gossip."

The good bits were that one of Glenn's teenage students had developed a massive crush on him, resulting in stupendous awkwardness at his school. Celine gave us the skinny on the boyfriend that caused her to flake on New Year's – a Nigerian dude named Adonis who owned one of the many "hip-hop stores" scattered throughout urban centers in Japan. No one had heard a peep from Chantelle, who hadn't shown up by that evening. We didn't want to entertain the notion that she'd gone for good, but our fears were confirmed by the LUNA coordinators. She'd left Japan, but they weren't at liberty to tell us why. We never did find out.

The week flew by. We watched our fellow teachers do demo lessons and traded valuable feedback during the days, and at night we either hit the bars or stayed at the training center playing drinking games. During one booze-ridden stretch of camaraderie on the last night, when it was just the three of us left in the common room, I let it slip.

"So, I started meditating."

Glenn, who'd been treating us to a chopsticks drum solo,

stopped short. "What, just now?"

Celine busted out laughing from where she'd been hogging the couch.

"No, genius," I said. "Back in Nagaoka."

"Oh, for real? You do it regularly?" he asked.

"Yep, pretty much every night."

"You feel any different?"

"Yeah, man. Way less stressed out. I thought I was losing it there for a while, but now I'm cruising. I can't believe it's been seven months already."

"That's like the best thing you can do for your mental health," Celine put in. Then she raised her glass. "I don't need it, though. I've got gin!"

"I did it for a while back in the day," Glenn went on. "But I could never get it into my routine, you know? Always felt good, though."

Celine stood up, stretched her arms towards the ceiling and sucked in a deep breath, then exhaled loudly as she bent down to touch her toes. She sat down again and crossed her legs, sober-looking as a nun.

"Was that like your magical detox maneuver?" I asked.

She threw me a little wink and ignored the question. "Jerry used to meditate," she said. "He told me he could see himself from outside his body sometimes. Pretty crazy."

A quiet moment passed.

"And Jerry would be…"

"My brother."

"I didn't know you had a brother!"

She shrugged. "Well, now you do. So are you gonna run off and join a monastery? Because I would totally support that life decision."

Glenn jumped to his feet. "Great idea! Much as I will now run off and join the toilet." He turned and was out the door.

Celine suddenly stood up again and grabbed me by the arm. "C'mere, you," she said, pulling me over to the corner. For one mad second I thought she was about to kiss me. She couldn't be *that* drunk.

A white box appeared from behind her back. "Here you go," she said, handing it to me.

"What's this?"

"It's called a present. Open it."

"Is it jewelry? I *love* jewelry!"

"Yes, it's jewelry. Open it."

"Oh my God, is it topaz earrings? Topaz is my birthstone! How'd you know?!?"

*"Open the fucking box!"*

Content that I'd sufficiently irked her, I cracked it open. Out leapt the loveliest aroma my unsuspecting nose had ever tasted. Filled with a sudden reverence, I carefully pulled out the box's contents. A large, round candle emerged, heavy in hand and gorgeous to the eye. Thin bolts of brown wax encircled a core of silver and white, dotted by air bubbles of various sizes just beneath the surface. Its base narrowed slightly at the middle before widening again at the top, where it was crowned by triple wicks.

"Wow," I whispered, turning it in my hand and lifting it up for a closer smell. I breathed deep. "What is that?"

"Sandalwood," Celine replied. "It's a tree that only grows in Asia. Adonis introduced me to it like a month ago and now I'm addicted. It's the best smelling thing ever."

I sniffed it again before slipping it back in its box. "Jesus, that is divine."

"Right? It's expensive too, so don't lose it."

"I won't. Man, now I feel bad I didn't get you anything."

"No, you don't."

"What's the occasion, anyway?"

"Eh, losing all those students must have been crappy. I thought this would cheer you up."

"Aww," I said, and I meant it.

"The guy at the candle shop makes all his stuff by hand. So he says, anyway. Enjoy!"

"You really *do* love me!" I threw my arms open and put on my cheesiest smile. "I think somebody gets a hug!"

She spun to an about-face, quite deliberately smacking me in the face with her ponytail. "Nope, I don't do hugs," she sighed, falling back onto the couch as Glenn reappeared and sniffed loudly.

"Somebody rockin' the sandalwood up in here?"

I got back to the business of meditating immediately upon my return to Nagaoka. The time off had actually made it easier, as if my brain muscles had been given time to heal up after a marathon. The familiar sensation of the muck flowing into my Bruce Lee fist put the whole world at ease, and I breathed out everything the Gremlin had been bitching about for the past week. That particular night, however, something different happened.

I'd developed a little ritual of starting each session by slamming my right fist into my left palm, in front of my face at eye level, as a symbolic little "cracking of the whip" to get the Gremlin's attention before muzzling it. Perhaps I did it with a bit of excessive force after a week-long hiatus, because a triangular shape roughly resembling the outline of my two hands suddenly popped into my mind's eye. It floated in the blackness of my closed eyes, but glowed with an orange light that seemed to shimmer in time with the music I had playing. I regarded it thoughtlessly, tickled by an odd sense of familiarity. Where had I seen this mystical orb before? Not that I actually cared. Everything about it felt friendly – a curious new visitor, both there and not there, hovering in front of me just beyond reach. Or was it miles away? Its aura hummed about its edges while some hidden source of gravity at its core, soft but inescapable, gently coaxed my mind towards it.

Was this just another distraction, or something else entirely? Had I dislodged some unknown aspect of consciousness hitherto concealed in the unexplored recesses of my mind? Yes or no, something told me to try projecting the muck outwards to it rather than down into my fist like before.

This was tricky at first; the little orb kept disappearing on me. But I could usually bring it back with a good fist slam, which had become my reflexive response whenever the Gremlin started yapping about jelly donuts or some other stupid thing.

By summer I didn't need my Bruce Lee fist to "conjure the orb," so I saved it for those lousy sessions where the Gremlin was extra loud. Plenty of things could trigger that – a bad day at work, depressing news from Iraq, not sleeping well the night before, computer issues, sore feet, or sometimes nothing at all. Not every session was a good one. But for the most part, I could sit down and get right to it, using my new little orb as a kind of visual mantra in which to encase the muck – *outside* my body. I had a feeling this was a milestone.

After a successful first year, Foreign Teachers are given the option to stay on for a second one. LUNA mails an updated contract and the FT checks one of two boxes at the bottom of the page: "YES, I will continue for another year" or "NO, I will not continue." With no longer any desire to leave, I checked the YES box and gave my contract to Manager to send to HQ.

A few weeks later I got a phone call at the school right after my last class. This never happened, so naturally the Gremlin started howling all the dreadful things that would happen when I said hello. I braced myself for bad news. Derek, one of LUNA's regional directors, was on the other end of the line. He asked me how I was doing, how classes were going, how I was getting along with Manager, and a few other pleasantries before getting to the bloody point.

"So, unfortunately," he began with a sigh, "it looks like someone put your contract in the NO pile. They just came to me with the error this morning."

fired at last. enjoy the flight back to baltimore.

"The problem is, we've already recruited another FT at the Nagaoka school," Derek said. "We sent them the recruitment packet and they've accepted the position, so at this point it's impossible for us to rescind the offer."

My fist tightened around the receiver as I fought the urge

to toss it out the window. My neck went limp and my chin hit my chest.

"What I can do, though, is offer you one of our Emergency Teacher positions next year."

**he didn't just say that.**

*Oh, but he did.*

The Emergency Teacher (ET) position was the Holy Grail for all Foreign Teachers at LUNA. These elite few were responsible for taking over for FTs who got sick, quit suddenly, or were otherwise unable to continue teaching. Whenever this happened, LUNA would deploy an ET as a short-term substitute, ensuring that the classes would go on. This meant that an ET might be sent to any one of over sixty branch schools throughout Japan, at any time, and had no idea what awaited them when they walked through the door. It was their charge to keep things in order until a new FT could be assigned.

It was no easy gig, as Derek explained. An ET had to be creative, tough, and flexible as hell. It certainly wasn't for everyone. But it also meant a salary bump, paid travel expenses, subsidized rent, and a way to see a whole lot more of the country. LUNA only had six of them.

"You don't have to start right away," Derek continued. "If you want to take some vacation after you leave Nagaoka, this would be the perfect time. You've got up to a month of unpaid leave before your new contract begins."

*Still think we should quit?*

My voice cracked like a thirteen-year-old pubescent boy as I strove to contain my elation. "That all sounds good to me. I'd love a month off if it's really no problem."

"Not at all," he said. "I'll make sure we make a note of it, correctly this time. Sorry again for the mix-up. I really appreciate your flexibility."

"No problem whatsoever! These things happen."

"Well, they really shouldn't. Calling to let you know personally was the least I could do."

"Much appreciated, Derek."

"Thanks, Matt. Have a good night."

The call disconnected with a click and I stood there holding the phone. Was I just promoted by administrative error? Am I getting pranked or something? Surely fate wouldn't hand-deliver a gift of such magnitude; no doubt the universe would strike me down to balance things out again. Of course, I didn't believe in that sort of thing, did I?

I floated back to my classroom and looked around with entirely new eyes, the walls blurred by a haze of impermanence. Giddiness welled up like a geyser and would have erupted if Manager hadn't popped her head in the door.

"Everything okay?" she asked.

I told her the news. She responded with wide eyes and a hand over her mouth.

"Congratulations, Matto sensei!" she beamed.


That evening I emailed all my friends back home, just in case someone might be passing by the Far East during my month off. It was worth a shot. A flurry of replies came from my nearest and dearest, ranging from openly jealous hostility to accusations of psychotic braggadocio. They all had merit, of course. Unfortunately, none of the old crew was likely to be in this hemisphere any time soon.

I gave Celine a call to tell her the news, and maybe rub it in her face just a little. However, my evil plan came to naught when she dropped her own bomb – she'd been promoted to ET and was staying another year herself! Apparently, she'd been a rock star teacher and sought out the position on her own merits. This came as little surprise, really. For all her tomfoolery, Celine had her shit together.

A few days later I was sifting through my email at the community center when a chat window from my high school buddy, Nima, popped up in the corner of my screen.

"Yo bro... gonna be in India with the fam in September. You're on vacation then, right? When are you off?"

"The ninth. When do you arrive?"

"The sixth. You should come."

I don't recall the rest of that conversation other than a curious look from the guy at the other computer as I jumped up and down.

India. The cradle of meditation. I'd never imagined such an opportunity would present itself in this lifetime. But there it was, knocking like a sledgehammer.


I expected my farewell to Nagaoka to be a lot more depressing, but the only thing on my mind was my upcoming trip. This diluted the sadness and my final day passed like any other. Hinako was the only student who expressed any emotion at all, ending our class with red, teary eyes and a great big hug. Yukiho, Takuma, and even Misaki wrote me adorable little thank-you notes, but most of the ungrateful twerps ran out with a barely a wave. Dinner with the JTs, some karaoke, a few photos, and that was it. It was all very professional. The most poignant moment was that last look at my apartment as I walked out the door.

# INDIA

Nima's dad turned 60 that year. An important milestone in the Hindu tradition, this birthday symbolized the transition away from earthly concerns towards those of the spirit. "A cosmic retirement party" is how Nima described it. The whole family would be returning to his dad's hometown in the south of India to celebrate with all their extended relations. Their plan was to fly into Delhi, rent a van and a driver, and visit a string of historical sites on their way south from the capital to their destination. It was essentially a month-long driving tour of the western half of the country, and it was Nima's job to sell his mom and dad on the idea of having my Irish Catholic ass tag along like an undeserving hobo. Since they'd already made all their arrangements, it was just a question of making the logistical adjustments necessary to accommodate one extra person for the first three weeks, which was all the time I could spare.

Mr. and Mrs. Patel had always liked me. I was a sobering influence on Nima's deviant behavior in high school, and I was much more polite to them than he ever was. He was kind of a mess as a teenager, courting drugs and alcohol just a bit too early, but he'd begun to turn things around by the time the two of us became friends. The timing of that was just a coincidence, but I was hardly inclined to downplay my role in his transformation while they pondered the idea of my riding with them across the subcontinent. I just hoped they went for it.

They did. In fact, they were delighted by the chance to show off their homeland to an outsider, even a bit surprised I was interested in visiting India in the first place. Not only did they invite me to join them, but they adjusted their itinerary around my burning desire to see the Taj Mahal. They hadn't included Agra in their circuit, but since I'd already declared to Nima that I wasn't leaving India without seeing it, his parents agreed this was the perfect opportunity to cross it off their bucket list. They'd never been.

My coolest passport stamp ever was the one that said *Embassy of India, Tokyo.* With excessive pride I passed it to the young lady at the check-in counter at Narita Airport.

"Destination?"

"Delhi."

The plane touched down eleven hours later at Indira Gandhi International Airport. I sailed through customs at miraculous speed and was met by many stares, fewer than during that very first hour in Japan but noticeably less friendly. Two uniformed soldiers with AK-47s stood by a set of double glass doors that exited out to the arrival area. I saw their weapons and my guard went up. Avoiding eye contact, I stepped past them and down a few steps into a small, colorless room chock full of people in transit. I looked around. There was no sign of the Patels.

Two currency exchange booths stood in the corner. The plan was to give Nima cash up front to cover my expenses for the next three weeks (pre-paid by his parents), including hotels, food, transportation, and the like. We'd worked it out beforehand to around $800. I stepped up to the glass and threw the young man on the other side the most charming smile I could muster. It was not returned. He couldn't have been older than seventeen.

I bent down and spoke into the circle of holes at neck level. "Good morning!" Was it morning? "I'd like to exchange 80,000 yen, please."

I passed eight ¥10,000 notes through the arch at the base of the glass. The kid gave me a quick, emotionless look before passing each one under a UV light. I waited patiently as he fiddled around under the counter. He then placed a three-inch-high stack of hard currency on the counter in front of me, as if tossing me my cut of last night's casino heist.

Before I could open my mouth to respond, my hand snatched up the cash pile and pocketed it, just to get it the hell out of sight.

"Is this right?" I asked in disbelief. The kid ignored me and kept on fiddling. He looked up again and his eyes drifted over my left shoulder. He froze.

A group of people were clamoring through the exit behind me, in clear sight of the extra-large cash transaction currently in progress. The young man eyeballed the crowd warily as it dispersed, then quickly passed me two more massive stacks of rupees, both as thick as the first. It was, by far, the largest mass of legal tender I'd ever seen. Once again my hands, quite a bit sweatier now, snatched them up and buried them in my clothes. I silently prayed that there was no more coming – I was fresh out of pockets.

The kid handed me a receipt and our business was concluded. I now bore enough cash to feed everyone in sight for about a month. I turned to face the world again, teeth clenched and awaiting my imminent murder.

nice one, dumbass. you just painted the world's biggest bulls-eye on your face.

I surveyed my surroundings. This arrival area was an imp compared to the thundering behemoths in Tokyo and Osaka. Assortments of relatively well-to-do-looking citizens occupied three rows of worn-out seating off to my left, while a mob of hungry-looking taxi drivers, all men, sniffed out their prey just beyond the glass doors leading outside.

Still no sign of the Patels. Granted, I'd passed through customs more quickly than anticipated. Perhaps they'd estimated a later exit time for me and were en route at this very moment.

or perhaps you're screwed.

A family of four was met by their arriving guest and a few precious seats were suddenly open. I bolted towards them and planted myself down with such a thud that one of my rifle-wielding soldier friends turned and shot me a soul-penetrating glare. I returned an "oops, silly me" sort of grimace and he turned away again, paying me no heed. Not so the people seated around me. I was being stared at. Sized up. Analyzed for weaknesses and the best method of attack. Everyone in this little room knew damn well what treasure lay buried in my trousers, ready for the taking. Somehow, they knew.

*Enough with the paranoia! Stay cool and everything else will be, too.*

A twinge in my ear dispelled the prophetic vision of doom – someone was speaking English behind me. I was about to turn around when my attention was diverted by two large, fast-moving objects. The soldiers had spun around to the doors they were guarding and flung them open, holding them ajar with the heels of their boots. A young man in gray shorts and a faded yellow t-shirt slowly crept through, pushing a wheelchair occupied by a woman who couldn't have been younger than 160. Dressed in a brilliant gold and purple sari, the ancient one raised her hand to the armed men, who smiled kindly back with a nod.

And with that, the most menacing element of the whole situation became the most reassuring. What was I thinking? I wasn't going to get robbed here, for God's sake. What kind of an idiot would try to start a ruckus with these two heroes keeping the peace? All I had to do was stay within eyeshot and they'd have my back for sure. My shoulders relaxed and I waited patiently for my friend to show up.

\* \* \* \* \*

"No luggage?" Nima said with a puzzled look when he appeared two hours later and we'd exchanged pleasantries. I gave my carry-on a little pat. The bulk of my belongings was safely tucked away in a locker back in Narita. "I travel light, amigo. Where's the fam?"

"Right there."

"Matt!" a woman cried. I recognized the voice from the thousand times in high school I'd heard it angrily thrown at her son. She pulled me into a hug and squeezed hard.

"Don't suffocate him, mom," Nima said.

Mr. Patel shook my hand with vigor. "Welcome, welcome! How was your flight?"

"As good as it gets!" I replied. "A smooth ride, decent food, and no delays. We landed right on time."

"You been waiting long?" Nima asked.

"Eh, like an hour or so."

"Whaaat?" he gaped as he grabbed my bag and we stepped out into the swarm of cabbies, who ambushed us on sight. Nima ignored them with great skill and shouted to be heard over the buzz of solicitations. "Sorry, man, that sucks! I thought it'd take a while for you to get your check-in and go through customs! Was there like no line?"

"None! I was amazed!"

Things quieted down as we worked our way to the far side of the mob, where an unmarked Mercedes van waited for us. By the driver's side stood a stocky, middle-aged man nursing a cigarette. He wore a pair of white earbuds and was lip synching to some joyous melody, eyes shut and fully committed. They popped open again as we approached. He yanked out the earbuds, reached through the open window and started up the van.

"That's Ravi," Nima said as the driver came around to meet us. "Ravi's our road warrior. Say hello to Matt, Ravi!" "Nice to meet you, my friend!" Ravi said as he took my bag from Nima. "First time in India?"

"First time!" I confirmed.

"Outstanding!" he replied as he tossed my bag into the enormous trunk and slammed it shut. Nima and I climbed into the back.

Spend an hour in Delhi and you'll never whine about traffic again. As we pulled out of the airport, we plunged into a maelstrom of human activity so thick and perilous it was almost comical. Cars were everywhere, zigging and zagging like hyperactive minnows in a frantic charge down the asphalt river. Adding to the mix were buses, bicycles, tuk-tuks, overflowing pickup trucks, whole families on mopeds, pedestrians, dogs, cattle, prowling taxis, young men hauling food carts, naked children mulling around, and the occasional high-end BMW. A collision of any two at any speed would be catastrophic, creating a ripple of destruction few would escape. And that was just the stuff that moved. Potholes, cracks, plates, dips, patches, puddles, and detritus littered the street beneath us, just itching to devour any unsuspecting tires that crossed their path.

"Good God," I muttered as I watched the chaos through the glass. I gave my seat belt a little tug for good measure.

"Crazy, right?" Nima said. "We're not even downtown yet." He crawled over to my window (he was never one to buckle up) and rolled it down to sample the audio. It was like opening the ark of the covenant.

The shriek of the concrete jungle rushed in to murder my eardrums – a deafening grinding sound that overwhelmed the airwaves as countless engines redlined and screeched to a halt again. Droves of people on foot buzzed around an unending line of shops, carts, and dwellings at the edge of the road, shouting at each other over the noise as they carried out their business. Not to mention the incessant beeping – not of the punitive sort we use in the West, but purely cautionary. Only a fool would assume any of the vehicles had working mirrors, so drivers would tap the horn in warning whenever they passed into someone's blind spot. It was just one of the rules of the road. Ravi followed it to the letter.

Nima rolled the window up and the scene was muted once again. "See all those cows?"

"Yeah, I was wondering about that. Don't people slam into them?"

"Nope. They just strut around in the middle of the street and people swerve to avoid them. They're all like, 'This is MY road, bitches!' It's a Hindu thing."

I had to laugh. "What, like Ganesh?"

"Ganesha. And dude, Ganesha's the elephant, not the cow. Get your shit straight, you wretched infidel!"

"Ah, shut yer filthy pagan hole."


I thought I'd seen poverty driving through some of the dodgier parts of Baltimore and D.C. Wrong again.

Mile after mile of indigence lay between the airport and downtown Delhi. Granted, neighborhoods around airports tend to struggle more than others, so I figured things would get better as we approached the city center. They didn't. The only difference was that tiny islands of immense wealth began to appear amidst the penniless ocean. Luxury outlets, high-end restaurants, and five-star hotels shared the streets with shanty towns and cardboard houses. The class divide was a chasm, the high and mighty dwelling side by side with the wretched of the earth. How did this powder keg of inequality not explode into revolution? There were no soldiers prowling the streets or gestapo on every corner. Hell, we didn't pass a single police car the entire ride.

It's not often you're hit with pity, anger, shame, disbelief, and gratitude all at once. The mix made my stomach churn. Nima shared my stunned silence – born and raised in mid-Atlantic USA, my Indian-American friend was just as much out of his element as I was. A couple of rich Westerners who'd never gone a day without as much hot food and clean water as we could stomach. Our shampoo was scented and our clothes were dried with fabric softener.

you really are a genuine piece of—

*No, we're just very, very lucky. Remember that.*

Nima's voice cut through the quiet. "I am so glad you guys got the fuck out of here." He was talking to his parents.

His dad leaned over from shotgun and eyed him in the rearview. "You don't have to swear like that, Nima."

"See why you should be more thankful?" his mom scolded from the lone middle-row seat by the sliding door. "Your generation doesn't appreciate anything."

We stopped at a red before a massive intersection. There

was a gentle tap on the window. A young girl stood outside, face caked in dust and wearing an expression of misery. I guessed she was about ten. She carried a naked baby and held it aloft.

As I reached into my pockets, Mrs. Patel turned and looked me dead in the eye.

"Never give to beggars," she said in a tone of iron. "Especially the children. Someone will see them get the money and rob them a minute later, very often with violence. Either that or they give the money to some criminal they work for."

The girl saw my face through the window and her eyes widened. She rounded on me, pressing the infant up against the glass next to my head. I groaned.

"That's not her baby." Mrs. Patel said in response.

"Huh?"

"They find abandoned children and use them to beg for money. When they get too old they just throw them away."

I groaned louder.

"Goddamn, are you serious?" Nima asked. His mom nodded as the light turned green and we pulled away.

"No swearing!" his dad protested from the front.

Nima and I exchanged a revolted look. "Remind me to never complain about anything ever again," he said.


I surrendered to the itinerary Mr. and Mrs. Patel had drawn up. Nima did, too. He worshipped spontaneity and insisted that this trip be one giant exercise in it. As such, he'd taken no part in the planning process and had no idea what we were in for, either.

We spent the first few days touring the capital as Ravi escorted us around to the attractions. There was no shortage of them. Great masterpieces of Mughal architecture loomed tall across the city, carrying the memory of the empire at the height of its power. The old Shahs were quite fond of constructing forts, mosques, and tombs for themselves and their queens as they expanded across the subcontinent. Hindu temples were everywhere as well, providing an enduring contrast of historical, religious, and architectural styles far older than anything my eyes recognized. The largest of these (in the world, in fact) was located just south of town. We took our time with that one, wandering the immense complex and marveling at the exquisite marble halls, shrines, statues, and artwork.

We were on the road again heading south bright and early on the fourth day. Nima and I entertained ourselves with a pocket-sized magnetic chess board he'd kept tucked away for road trips. I'd always considered my prowess at the game to be respectable, but after four straight losses my friend had convinced me otherwise. We called it quits when one of the little rooks disappeared between the seat cushions. Our brains were fried eggs by that point, anyway – four games is pushing it.

"So tell me more about Japan," Nima sighed, tossing the board into his backpack and returning to a slouching position.

I leaned back into my seat and kicked off my shoes, wondering why the devil I'd been wearing them this whole time. "Alright, whaddaya wanna know?"

"I dunno, just tell me about it. What do you do when you're not teaching?"

"Eh, not a whole lot, man. The job is pretty all-consuming. Occasionally I'll head down to Tokyo on the weekend to hit the clubs with my buddy, Glenn."

"That's pretty slick, what's that guy like?"

What an interesting question. How *does* one describe an entire person in a sound bite? "He's kinda like you, actually," I said. "Less of an asshole, of course."

"Right on," Nima replied, unfazed. "You find yourself a cute little Japanese girlfriend yet?"

"Nah, still workin' on that one," I said. A twinge of embarrassment nibbled at me. "I don't actually hang out with many Japanese people."

"Seriously?"

"I know, it's lame. That's the one thing I'm most disappointed about."

"So, go make some friends!" Nima replied, as if it were the easiest thing in the world. "You're a sociable dude. You're way more outgoing than I am."

"Dude, I have ZERO energy at the end of the day. Even on the weekends all I want to do is chill out and recharge the batteries."

"What do you get up to during the week?" he asked.

"Very little. Watch movies, play guitar, keep a journal, hit the bottle. Meditate."

He perked up at that last bit. "For real?"

"Yep, every night. Well, almost every night."

"No shit? Is it working?"

"Yeah, man. I feel totally different." I was suddenly dying to talk about it. "Dude, when I meditate... it's just like..." I passed a hand across my face, as if wiping the whole world away.

"Totally!" Nima beamed. "It's awesome you're doing that, man. I wish you'd told me! You have to read this."

He rummaged around his backpack, pulled out a beaten-up old paperback and handed it to me. On the cover was a photo of a little stone path running through a patch of forest. *Tao Te Ching,* by Lao Tzu. I turned it over to read the blurb on the back.

"Each page is a different verse with a different message, sort of like poetry but not really," Nima said. "You know the yin yang? It came from this book. You can keep it, I have another copy at home."

I read the first verse. "The Tao," I muttered at the end.

"It's basically this old Chinese philosopher's idea of God from like two thousand years ago," Nima replied. "More or less. Not exactly. Just read it."

Reading in a moving vehicle always gave me a headache, so I slammed the book shut and stuffed it in my bag. "Dude, you know I can't read. Why you gotta rub it in my face?"

"Shut up."

I'd been half-asleep all morning and barely noticed the van pulling off the road and stopping. Nima and I hopped out to stretch our cramped limbs, eagerly awaited an early lunch. There was nothing different about the river of people that swarmed all around us here – crowds were inescapable in India – except these folks were amassed around a large red trailer that vaguely resembled a ticket booth.

After scanning the chaotic scene before us, Mrs. Patel turned to her son and me. "Boys, you wait here." She crossed the street and was swallowed up by the crowd.

"Uh, Dad?" Nima uttered. "Should she be doing that?"

"Oh, yes," his dad replied. "She likes to haggle."

Nima shot me a confused look and shrugged. "Seems like kind of a sketchy place to get food."

"No, you cannot eat here," Mr. Patel replied with a grin. She returned a few minutes later and handed Nima a small, white sheet of paper. He looked at it for a split second, then shot his head up and looked around wildly. "Oh shit, are we here?"

She handed me a yellow one and smiled. "I tried to get you the discount for local people, but they saw you with us. You are too tall and too white to hide!"

I looked down at what she'd given me. Amidst a mass of faded Hindi text, two English words leapt from the paper like bottle rockets – TAJ MAHAL. The chills up and down my spine masked the intense heat of the day.

"Let's hurry while it's still early," Mrs. Patel said, now all business. She turned to her husband. "Did you eat something?"

"Yes, yes."

"Good. Boys, grab some water."

The front of the complex was built so that visitors entered through a dark, narrow archway that masked what lay beyond. As we stepped across the threshold, an enormous courtyard opened up before us with an almost alarming suddenness. It must have covered a full square mile, as if transplanted there by some supernatural force. All the chaos of downtown Agra – the mass of people, the grinding traffic, the incessant beeping, barking, and shouting – faded at once to a solemn quiet. Voices turned to whispers. Brown dirt became green grass. Apartment buildings and canopy jungle yielded to an azure open sky. The landscaping was dotted by short, perfectly-trimmed green trees that reminded me of over oversized *bonsai.* Huge, red stone structures stood far off to the right and left like giant sentries guarding the path forward. But these were dwarfed by the centerpiece directly ahead.

Dominating the scene like a white flame in the darkness, there stood the living image of a thousand romantic postcards. My eyes were helpless to resist its gaze. A long, narrow reflecting pool extended out from its base towards us, flanked by wide strips of low-cut grass and red stone walkways on either side. The still air teased an aroma of burning incense.

"Jesus Christ," I let fall from my gaping mouth.

Nima grabbed me by the shoulders and put on a ridiculously overblown Punjabi accent. "You will find no Jesus here, my Christian friend!"

I snapped out of my trance and reached for my camera, clicking away madly alongside dozens of hypnotized visitors. For some reason people kept asking *me* to take pictures of them. I was happy to oblige. Nima's parents were no exception – the childish wonder on their faces made for a great photo.

We continued forward, relenting to the flow of people moving in a mellow stream towards the base of the Taj. It wasn't until we were up close that the full majesty of the architecture revealed itself. I could hear the breath stolen from my lungs.

The mausoleum sat atop a massive marble plinth at least thirty feet high. Twin stairwells allowed pedestrian access to the top of it. Shoes were not permitted, of course, so we kicked ours off and tucked them into one of the hundreds of cubby holes on hand for that purpose. The fresh air through my socks felt wonderful; the white stone beneath them was surprisingly cool given the intensity of the sun. My feet touched marble and my mind went blank. No doubt this was an automated response to sheer amazement as the perception of millennia of history took over. Here I stood, some 23-year-old American slugabed, upon the crown jewel of one of mankind's most ancient civilizations. It was all too much – my brain bid me the ol' AOL *goodbye* and just logged out.

All remaining sound faded as I climbed the steps to the top of the plinth. The mausoleum towered overhead, boasting its true enormity for the first time. The great central dome was barely visible looking up from this close. Colossal, arched recesses were carved out around the façade, each shaped like the overturned hull of some massive cruise ship. Intricate floral motifs, abstract patterns, and flowing Arabic calligraphy were etched into their edges. Black, red, and blue inlaid stone provided a stark contrast to the white marble, whose naturally occurring color variations provided their own subtle flair. Four towering minarets leapt to the heavens from the four corners of the plinth, standing like great lighthouses amidst an ocean of clear sky.

I reached out and pressed my fingertips against the stone. It was real. I was actually here.

Impossible. The Taj Mahal was mythical, fantastic. Like so many of earth's wonders, it only existed in magazines, movies, and web sites. My trite little life and this far-off place had no intersection. How could they? This was the domain of famous explorers and warrior kings, not some bozo like me. The Taj Mahal? Nothing but a picture. There was never a scrap of reality to it.

Yet here I was, touching it with my living flesh. I stood there in a stupor, blackout drunk on personal triumph. I could very well have been drooling all over myself. More likely there were tears on my face.

*No place on earth is out of our reach.*

My caress turned aggressive and I slapped down as hard as I dared. The marble scoffed in response, smarting my fingers with the staying power of its unyielding superstructure. I leaned forward to smell the stone, hoping to detect the lingering scent of passing centuries, but I couldn't smell a thing. I chuckled at my own folly and stepped inside.

The interior was more cramped than I'd imagined. The designs across the exterior façade had continued inwards, though in smaller, denser proportions. The tomb of the Shah who'd commissioned its construction (and that of his late wife who'd provided the inspiration) lay hidden in a closed-off chamber below. What was open to the public here at ground level were mere replicas of the true graves. The two false sarcophagi in the center were nonetheless heavily adorned, appearing as twin rectangular altars atop wide, flat pedestals and surrounded by an octagonal gate that prohibited direct contact. The smaller of the two lay directly in the center of the room, while the larger one, the only asymmetric element in the whole chamber, lay next to it. Floral patterns, inlaid once again in dark stone, decorated every inch of their surfaces.

Stepping outside again and dazzled anew by the gardens all around, I realized I had no idea where the Patels had gone. I'd been completely lost inside myself. There must have been a thousand visitors that morning and not a trace of them had registered in my brain. My crew was close by, of course, each living the experience in their own way. Connecting again, the four of us re-entered tourist mode and basked in our mutual delight. We stayed at the Taj for a long time, snapping all the essential photos, doing slip-'n'-slide on the marble floors (I nearly face-planted several times), and drinking the whole place in. And, naturally, I found a quiet patch of grass to meditate for a while. It was quite a backdrop.

Our path from Agra led us southward towards the town of Udupi, with numerous stops along the west coast of the country. The Patels were natural tour guides, bringing the van to a halt every few hours to explore other sites of historical and spiritual significance. I rode my first pachyderm, ate mystery meals off banana leaves, and time and again learned the true meaning of humidity. I breathed in enough incense to contract emphysema and sweat enough bricks to build a castle. I drenched myself in sunblock, Axe body spray, and mosquito repellant. By some miracle I even managed to avoid the ravages of Delhi belly.

I offered to reciprocate the hospitality to the Patels if they were ever inclined to explore Japan, knowing full well that they, like everyone else back home, would not be. But hey, good manners are good manners.

"Hit me up when you're stateside again, man," Nima said back in the capital as the taxi driver tossed my bag in the trunk. Three weeks of vacation had passed like three minutes.

"Yeah, dude, you'll have to fill me in on what I missed!"

"Ah, it'll just depress you. Fucking Republicans keep trying to –"

"Okay, I'm outta here!" I interrupted. I gave him the same farewell hug I'd given his parents a few minutes before.

"Read that book, man." Nima said through the open window as I climbed into the back seat. "You'll dig it."

"That's why God invented planes!" I replied with a final peace sign. The cab lurched forward and was engulfed by the churning river of man, beast, and machine that flowed out of the city towards the airport.

My flight back to Osaka was "delayed" for thirty hours due to a faulty cabin door. It was a wretched fiasco involving a rickety bus, a cheap hotel, and 160 irate passengers. But eventually the madness resolved itself and I was airborne at last, headed back home to begin the next phase of my grand adventure.

wait, did he just refer to japan as home?

*Sure did. How 'bout that?*

# THE WAY OF FIRE

My first destination as an Emergency Teacher was a city called Matsumoto. The town boasted one of the biggest castles in Japan, and there was a near-perfect balance of rural and urban about the place. My new apartment was older and smaller than the one in Nagaoka, but I'd become quite the light traveler – I only had my one suitcase, laptop, DVD case, guitar, and Celine's candle. Plus, my new place struck me as special somehow. It just felt more Japanese.

It hit me when I stepped into the living room and my toes cried out in wonder. Beneath them lay wall-to-wall *tatami* – traditional woven straw flooring. Pure Japanese style, not like that hardwood Western nonsense back in Nagaoka. I pulled off my socks and knew I was in love. That night I was overcome with the desire to bond with my new digs and get back to meditating, which I'd only done once that whole time in India. The *tatami* was perfect for it. Plus, an edginess crept in when I went too long without meditating, as if all the things that didn't matter in life were trying to re-assert their phony importance. The aroma of sandalwood engulfed my senses as I lit Celine's candle for the first time and got down to business.

I was rusty. The Gremlin jabbered with a ferocity I thought I was rid of at that point. Lack of practice does bad things to both body *and* mind, apparently. Thoughts came in from every which way, poking and prodding, slipping in uninvited from all corners of my unconscious. Memories of India, anxiety about my new ET role, curiosity about the city, and the anticipation of new students swarmed like mosquitos. So, I conjured the orb and started swatting them away. Bruce Lee fists flew fast and furious.


The lobby of my new school buzzed with activity the next morning. Children were everywhere, and their batteries were charged to max. The floor shook with sporadic tremors as dozens of little feet thundered about. High-pitched cries of *Matto sensei!* burst from unfamiliar mouths all around as I walked through the door – my coming had obviously been foretold. A streak of black hair and white uniforms suddenly rushed in my direction, flying past me and into the classroom over my shoulder.

"Hello, Matt sensei," the woman behind the front desk greeted me in a robotic tone. "Welcome. I am Masako, the manager. Thank you for coming. Your schedule is right here."

She passed me a single sheet of paper – a week's worth

of hand-written days, times, names, and levels. "Your classroom is right behind you," she said as the phone rang. "Good luck!" She picked it up and paid me no more heed.

I took a deep breath and turned to face the crucible. My first class consisted of six eight-year-old boys.

Well, this is going to royally suck.

Four of the six lads had taken their seats at the table, barely making a sound and plotting no evil. The two at the far end were jittery, though, fidgeting about with no intention of participating. I paid no attention to them. That was my first mistake.

A leader must assert dominance over the herd at the earliest possible opportunity. Even if no one is doing anything overtly disruptive, mischief in the classroom is an infection that never fails to fester. Discipline for discipline's sake is often necessary for assuming control. In other words, you've got to seize upon the first moment to show 'em who's boss. Think of it as breaking in a month-old labradoodle. If you want him to eat on command one day, you'll have to spend some time denying him food at first. Did the puppy do something wrong? Of course not. Does it feel good to do it? Quite the opposite. Does it ultimately contribute to a healthy environment? Damn right it does. Children are no different – they're all a bunch of labradoodles. The only difference in getting them to fall in line is that you don't use a leash.

All lessons not yet learned on Matsumoto day one. I slogged through that first class focusing on the good guys up front, hoping their influence would rub off on the other two dunces and the problem would correct itself. The opposite happened – the corruption spread. The outbursts at the far end of the table became more frequent. Pencils were spun and cards were thrown. My four allies, once seated at rapt attention, now turned their heads to be entertained by the spectacle unfolding in the back. The apprehension of a new teacher vanished from their faces as they tested the limits of my leniency.

And I let all the naughtiness slide, victimized by my own wishful thinking. I'd arrived wanting nothing more than to be the fun-filled, cool substitute teacher all the children loved to pieces, not one of those short-tempered, grumpy ol' farts I remembered from my own school days. The problem was, I appeared to be stuck in a repeated cycle of substitutitis – a rare but debilitating condition in which your students are incapable of giving two shits about you because they know you'll soon be old news. Lesson planning was futile, in-class activities were chaos, and no one was learning anything. And having my worst class first thing on Monday morning was an extra little kick to the head. By the end of the second week I wanted to throttle every last one of them.

"Oh God, I would *never* put up with that shit in my class," Celine said when I called her up that Friday night to vent. "You need to bring the thunder. Put the fear of the Almighty into the little brats, and do it right away."

"I mean, I don't want to actually *scare* them," I replied. She paused. "Why not?"

"Mostly because I don't want any of them to break down and start crying off to Mommy," I said. "That's the nightmare scenario."

"Come on," she scoffed. "You said they were like eight years old, right? And all boys? That'll never happen."

THE WAY OF FIRE

"It might."

"Only if you take it too far. You don't want to scream or anything – that'll just make it worse. You just gotta make them think you might literally be a crazy person capable of murder, and that one wrong move will set you off. Watch how well they behave if they think you're some explosive lunatic barely keeping his shit together."

"God, I miss you."

"Whatever. Just drop little hints that you may be insane. The next time one of them acts up, do something completely unexpected and unsettling."

"Like punch him in the face? No one would expect that."

"Ha! Oh, man, that would be so awesome."

"Like what, then?" I asked.

"I dunno. They're your students, not mine. But give them a little taste of your dark side and they'll totally fall in line. Just be sure to go back to normal like right away."

I mulled over our conversation that weekend while riding aimlessly around town. I had my doubts as to whether I could put Celine's plan into motion, but then I twisted my ankle on the way to the school Monday morning and instantly went into the red.

that's it, someone dies today!

*Easy there, killer. Let's try this another way.*

Patience at zero and foot throbbing, I walked into my classroom two minutes late and took my seat at the head of the table. My gaze went straight off into the distance as I took a deep, cleansing breath. The orb glistened in my mind's eye. The boys played their regular roles for a minute or two before I found myself on my feet again, powering through the pain and calm as a mountain lake. I picked up my chair, walked around and slammed it down hard at the foot of the table. Everyone jumped. I quietly sat down again, inches away from my two little headaches.

I turned and locked eyes with the troublemaker to my left. He stared back in surprise for maybe two seconds. My eyes narrowed slightly and his own dropped to his lap. I went right on glaring at him, then slowly turned my head to the right. Troublemaker number two must have seen it coming; he was already looking at his feet. I stared at him anyway, cracking a knuckle for effect.

Then I smiled and started class. I had six perfect little gentlemen for the next 45 minutes.

That was the first time I'd ever wielded the power of an awkward silence; an experiment that exceeded my most optimistic projections. From that moment the way forward was etched in stone. Celine was absolutely right, loud and angry was no good. Quiet and menacing was the ticket. These kids had no idea who I was or what I was capable of – all they had to do was fear the worst and they fell right in line. Heck, their English wasn't half bad once they quit screwing around. I even caught them enjoying themselves once or twice.

I made a mental note to be a bit nicer than usual to my two victims after class when we were all back out in the lobby, giving them wide smiles and high-fives of special flamboyance.

Never let a student leave thinking you're still mad at them.

My whole approach to teaching got flipped on its head as an ET. To hell with the curriculum, there was no time for it. I embraced a much simpler mission: size up where the students were language-wise and focus on fixing their worst habits.

Under normal circumstances, for example, a language teacher will almost never devote an entire lesson to pronunciation. I started doing it all the time. Always dropping your pronouns? Not today you aren't. Can't get your mouth to vibrate for a proper *"v"* sound? Gimme an hour, we'll get that squared away. Those crucial little differences between so-so English and good English were the stars I orbited.

I also had a new motto: age appropriate be damned. In Matto sensei's class you learned blackjack, beer pong, and Texas Hold'em. No money and no beer made no difference, my lessons were *fun*. This was the ultimate weapon – if the activities were entertaining enough so that the kids actually wanted to do them, incorporating English into them was a breeze. All I had to do was follow one rule like the First Commandment: the fun stopped dead in its tracks until the English was spot-on perfect. No one ever saw the river card with bad grammar. Too bad if the house was showing ten, you stood on thirteen if your prepositions were off. Double the blinds? Double the vocabulary.

The bad habits melted away and everyone started sounding better. Better still, the parents finally saw progress. It was common after a class for Mommy to ask for a run-down of what we'd learned that day, and the kids and I would give a little demo. Their child's improvement elated them, which delighted the students. Impressing the parents is *very* important to the Japanese, which is a big reason why the kids work so hard. I was happy to make it just a bit easier for them.

Celine's candle burned so often it had melted down to the nub. Since it wasn't coming with me to Nagano where I was headed next, on my last night in Matsumoto I gave it a little send-off by watching it burn out to oblivion while I meditated before bed. It had been a truly handsome chunk of wax. By that time, however, the poor thing was a blob of mud. I lit it up, cued the music and stared at the flame, reflecting on how much I'd miss that delightful smell. This was right around 10:00 p.m.

Then the clock read 12:48.

Wait... what?

I blinked hard and looked again. 12:49. That couldn't be right. Had I nodded off? I didn't think so; I hadn't tipped over. Wait, was I asleep right now and dreaming this entirely? Nope, definitely awake. As far as my neck could tell, my head hadn't even been bobbing. I also knew what falling asleep felt like, and this wasn't it. So how had I lost nearly three hours? I wasn't even meditating – no Bruce Lee fist, no orb, nothing.

The time had just vanished.

I picked up my iPod. Thirty-seven songs had played. It might as well have been a thousand. The candle, miraculously still ablaze, was a sputtering pool of liquid wax. I blew it out for the last time and went to bed expecting to feel like crap the next morning. I had to be up at 6:00 to catch the train to Nagano.

I woke up from my meager five hours of sleep utterly refreshed, buzzing with energy and ready to attack the day.

Since when does time just disappear like that? Could I make it happen again? I dissected the experience in my head over and over on the bullet train. The only thing I'd done differently than the other hundred times I'd meditated was to give my undivided attention to the candle burning. Maybe the presence of an open flame had changed something.

I'd always been mesmerized by fire. We all are, to some degree. Who among us can look at a blazing campfire, casting warmth and light in defiance of the cold night, without feeling that familiar wave of reverent serenity? With me it went just a bit deeper. Like borderline pyro deeper – tending a fire was practically a spiritual experience for me. I totally understood why some cultures worshipped it. By the time I arrived in Nagano I was convinced it was Celine's candle that had sparked that little time warp last night.

My stint there would be brief – a mere two weeks – which meant I was staying in a hotel rather than the last FT's apartment. There was no one waiting for me at the station to welcome me to my new life this time, just a long line of taxis and their chain-smoking captains.

The hotel room was minuscule but spotless. I checked in, dumped my bags, and immediately headed out to find the *Ito Yokado* (the Japanese Walmart) I passed on the ride over. It was a wonderful store that sold everything under the sun. I walked out with a hefty blue and black candle with a little plastic Buddha head attached around the perimeter by a thin strip of brown leather. It was a far cry from the sandalwood masterpiece I'd had before, but still pretty nifty as candles go.

Back at the hotel my suspicions were confirmed. I couldn't believe how quickly my mind went quiet just watching that thing burn. The rituals of the past were at once obsolete; a flame flickering in a dark room was a more potent orb than anything I could conjure in my head. It pulled the thoughts right from my mind and consumed them. I didn't have to push or swat them away, they simply fell into the light and went up in smoke. My Bruce Lee fist relaxed and I began resting my hands on my knees palms up, forefingers and thumbs gently pressed together like those nitwits in the Prozac commercials. Instead of capturing the Gremlin in a cage, I was now casting it into the fire... and the Gremlin *hates* fire.

I'll never know if my progress would have been quicker had I used a candle from the very beginning. Could the hypnotic power of fire have tamed the Gremlin so easily when it was truly ravenous during those first months in Nagaoka? Had I needlessly taken the long, rocky road up the mountainside, oblivious to the gondola right beside me?

No, I didn't think so. If I could start all over I would probably bust out the fire from the get-go, but something tells me it wouldn't have had its full level-ten effect if I hadn't climbed steps one through nine first. It was, after all, only a wee little flame.

From then on I always had a candle close by. It became the ultimate accessory, the burning center of my meditation space, the orb taken physical form to be called upon at need.

Fire made meditation effortless.

# KURASHIKI WINTER SICKNESS

Two figures bundled up in puffy coats, hats, and matching pink scarves waited for me at the bottom of the escalator as I made my way down from the platform at Kurashiki station, where I was stationed next. I could tell they were both female from their statures, but their winter apparel hid every scrap of skin. The one on the right went to her toes and waved at me – one of those big, sweeping ones you'd give a passing cargo ship if you were stranded on an island somewhere. She broke away from her counterpart and approached me with an outstretched arm. Her gloves matched her scarf.

"You're Matt sensei?" she asked as our hands clasped.

"That's me!" I said, trying to sound cheerful through my frozen face.

"I'm Haruna. This here is Silvia," she continued as the other caught up. "She's our other superstar FT!"

Silvia gave a quick wave, then folded her arms again as a gust of freezing wind crashed into us. We hurried over to where Haruna's car was parked nearby. The two of them climbed into the front and Haruna turned it over immediately to blast the heat. I threw my suitcase in the back seat and sat down next to it. I'd decided back in Matsumoto that my guitar was more trouble than it was worth, so I'd left it behind as a little welcoming gift to the incoming FT. I never found out if it was appreciated.

I'd never heard of Kurashiki before and it wasn't on any tourist map. Like Nagaoka, it had the look and feel of one gigantic suburb. It also had something in the air that set my allergies off almost immediately, made no more pleasant by the frigid winter. It was my home for the next six weeks.

"God, I can't stand this weather," Haruna said. My ears perked up when she said this – something exotic was hiding in her accent. Whatever it was, I wanted to hear more of it. She ripped off her gloves and rubbed her hands in front of the vent. Silvia did the same.

"I like your gloves!" I said, trying to coax more words out of her.

Silvia pointed silently at her colleague.

"I made those!" Haruna declared.

"The scarves, too," Silvia replied, waving the end of hers over her shoulder.

Haruna beamed through the rear-view. "And the scarves!"

The station wasn't far from the apartment, but there was a baffling abundance of traffic lights between them. Winter accessories came off one by one as the car warmed up and I got a better look at my two new co-workers. Haruna was darker than most of the Japanese people I'd met, with straight brown hair that curled forward as it ended at her shoulders. Her high cheek bones supported a pair of wire-framed glasses that bobbed up and down on her face when she spoke, which was often. She barely stopped for breath as she bared her soul to Silvia about the latest drama between her and her boyfriend.

Silvia was more petite and fair-skinned, with auburn hair worn in a style identical to Haruna's. She spoke little and never smiled, listening quietly to the saga unfolding from the driver's seat and offering only the occasional word of agreement or thoughtful nod. I could tell she was only feigning interest.

At the fifth or sixth light there was a pause in the story and the opportunity finally presented itself. I leaned forward. "Haruna sensei, where did you learn English?"

"I went to university in Perth," she answered with two thumbs up.

Never heard of it. "Where is that?"

"It's way out on the west coast of Australia. The only real city on that side of the country."

"Really? What's it like, mate?"

"Uh oh," Silvia cut in. "Don't get her started."

"I know!" Haruna laughed. "I'll talk all day about it. I could spend the rest of my life there."

I heard it at last when she said *life,* which carried through the air like a songbird. An Australian Japanese accent – how many people could show off one of those? It was wildly attractive.

137

"Right here!" Silvia suddenly blurted out, pointing to a rapidly-approaching driveway at ten o'clock. The seat belt attacked my collarbone at the sudden deceleration, while my brain leapt to the right side of my skull with the force of a hard left turn taken too quickly. I heard the tires peel. Never a good sign.

The vehicle came to a stop with one final lurch forward and the three of us shared a terrified silence. Silvia shot a hard look at Haruna, who wore a guilty expression.

"Sorry."

good god! way to reinforce the stereotype, lady!

Silvia held her stare. "You have got to slow down, honey. I don't want to fear for my life every time I get in your car."

"Sorry."

With an exasperated sigh Silvia threw the door open and stepped out. I thought she would slam it shut again, but to my surprise she closed it quite gingerly. "Thanks for the ride," I said as I followed her.

Haruna's smile returned. "You're welcome! I'll see you in the morning, mate!"

We stood outside a featureless, five-story apartment building, the only large structure in the vicinity. Silvia had already made a dash for the door and was holding it open for me. I stepped into the lobby, which consisted of little more than two elevators, a bench, and a wall of mailboxes. But it was warm. Gloriously warm. Both elevator doors stood ajar at the far end and I followed Silvia into the one on the right. She slapped the button for the fifth floor and stood there without a sound.

"Man, that wind is killer," I said.

"I know," she muttered through a kind of passive-aggressive sigh. "It's been like this all month."

The doors opened again and she led me down an open-air hallway, exposed to the winter again but at least shielded from the wind. We stopped at the first door on the right and Silvia gave it a quick tap with her knuckles. "This one's yours," she said.

I pointed at the doorknob. "How do I, uh…?"

"Oh, shoot," she answered, yanking Haruna's pink gloves out of her inside pocket. She reached in and pulled out a key ring with three keys on it. "Here. The big one is for the apartment and the little ones are for your mailbox and your bike."

"Thanks. So, is the school close by?"

"You don't know where the school is?"

"No idea."

"Manager didn't call you or anything?"

I shook my head.

"Figures," Silvia groaned. "I thought she'd at least come give you a ride, but I guess not. Be ready to go at 7:00, okay?" She turned and started back towards the elevator. "And dress warm. It's far."


The apartment was absurdly large. Normally this would be a good thing, but since I had so few possessions there was a lot of empty space that served no purpose. Fortunately, one of the previous occupants had had the good sense to adorn the living area with a giant, fuzzy brown rug. It was nice and soft and plenty thick. Really tied the room together.

The thing felt amazing. So much so that I couldn't resist stretching out like a cat and making a big, fluffy rug angel.

After a while I sat up again and tried to touch my toes. I made it to just past my knees. I stretched and I whined and I pouted like a little girl – my torso was about as flexible as a skateboard deck. And oh, how a wee spot of pain will set the mind roaring! I envisioned a thousand knives inflicting a thousand wounds on my poor, innocent hamstrings. Images of muscles shredding and tendons snapping danced about my mind's eye as the Gremlin howled at me to stop this madness immediately. My entire backside, from my shoulders to my ankles, burned like hell. Pretty sad. I only managed to stretch like this for about a minute.

This rigidity was unacceptable. We're made of soft flesh and bendy sinews, not brick and mortar for God's sake. I stretched like this again and again over the course of the next half hour or so, writhing every time. But I kept at it. I was already taking the time to make my mind healthier, so why not throw in a little something for the body, too? It wasn't like it took a whole lot of time, and I sure as hell had the space for it.

At the end of that very first stretch-a-thon I felt like I'd gone six rounds with Lennox Lewis. I had a long, long way to go before I began my career as a contortionist. I got into bed feeling sore, weak, and shaky, then promptly rolled over and slept like a corpse.


I should have dressed warmer. Silvia and I left the building on our bikes at 7:05 a.m. and collided with a brick wall of winter, following a path beside a long, straight road four lanes wide. On and on it went, slightly uphill, flanked by nothing but apartments on either side. I'd have called it a highway but for the lack of traffic. Lord only knows where it led.

Silvia led the charge at full speed, undeterred by the hostile elements. I followed close on her tail at first, but began to lag behind as the weather took its toll on body and soul. The steady climb was murder on my legs, searing my quads as the merciless wind froze my vital organs. The way went forward like this for a good fifteen minutes before we finally banked left at the first traffic light. I tried to take visual cues so I could navigate back after work, but nothing about this frozen town stood out to my watery eyes. I gave up after the third or fourth forgotten turn, vowing to make someone draw me a map instead.

At last Silvia came to a stop, slamming her ride into a metal bike rack and locking the rear wheel down in a single deft motion. I followed suit far more clumsily. Before us was a wide, one-story building with huge windows adorned with LUNA posters, flyers, and other promotional materials. Obviously the right place.

"Holy cow, you do this every day?" I asked Silvia as we stepped inside. My voice shook from the cold.

"Every goddamn day," she replied.

We hung our coats on a rack by the door and I felt the spark of life returning to my extremities. The lobby was empty and there was a strange gloom in the atmosphere. The only sound was that of a muted conversation in Japanese coming from the room behind the front desk. I walked over and poked my head through the doorway.

It was no bigger than a walk-in closet. Four women were gathered around one of the folding rectangular tables used to seat small children in the classroom. Ceiling-high, steel bookcases full of texts, binders, and other office materials lined every wall, resulting in an inescapably cramped feeling. The four JTs were busy at work gathering materials and writing up their lesson plans for the day. They stopped in their tracks when Silvia and I appeared. Only one of them smiled.

"Morning, Matt sensei!" Haruna said.

"*Ohayo gozaimasu!*" the other three echoed. I responded in kind.

"No Manager?" Silvia asked.

Haruna shook her head. "She's supposed to be in later, but who knows?" She scooted over to make a space for Silvia and me to join them in the minuscule workspace.

"Typical," Silvia grunted, dropping her backpack on an empty chair. Then she turned to me. "I guess I'm giving you the tour, then." We made our way down the corridors lined by empty classrooms, Silvia pointing them out in turn with palpable disinterest. The finale was the bathrooms directly across from the big classroom by the front door, where we ended up after our third right turn. It was the only one with a window.

"Thrilling," I said. "No trampoline?"

"Not exactly," Silvia replied. "Boss lady isn't the type."

"I see. So, which of these sacred domains is mine?"

"Oh, you don't have your own classroom."

I waited for the punchline.

"None of us do," she continued. Manager doesn't want any of the teachers using the rooms except during a class.

"You're kidding me."

She gave a contemptuous little laugh. "No, I'm not."

"So where do you work? Where do you plan lessons and make materials and all that?"

"Over there in the break room, where everyone is now. We spend half the day smushed in there, trying to not to drive each other crazy and waiting for Manager to come and yell at us."

This was unreal. "She actually yells?"

"Sometimes. Either that or she'll just chew us out for something dumb. Happens every day."

"Wow," was all I could say.

"She'll be nice to you, though."

"Why is that?"

"Because you're a man," she said, and walked back to the break room. Instead of following her I stepped into the big classroom. The big window let in heaps of natural light and offered advanced warning of anyone approaching the front door. A large alphabet poster, always handy, was taped to the wall and a wide assortment of colorful magnets stuck to the whiteboard. A bookcase in the corner carried every title in the LUNA portfolio. It was a pleasant, tidy, and well-maintained little space – a fine place to work.

I returned to the break room. Silvia was seated at the table now and a little nook had been carved out for me in front of an empty chair. It was more cramped than ever – my workspace was the size of a fast-food tray.

"Your schedule is there," Haruna said, pointing to a sheet of paper on the table. I picked it up, then pointed over my shoulder with my thumb.

"I'm gonna go work in that room."

My new colleagues looked at me as if I'd just confessed to killing a man. Nobody said a word as I grabbed my backpack and stepped out. I pulled up a chair and sat in the center of my newly claimed territory, sprawling my belongings as widely as I could across the table. I glanced at my schedule – my first class wasn't until noon. It was also a lesson I'd done a dozen times before, so there was no need to prepare in advance. I gazed out the window at the frosty winter morning for a while, clearing my head in typical fashion. The sound of quickened chatter from the break room carried across the hallway as I saw the first student of the day scamper towards the entrance.

An hour later Silvia appeared at my door. "All settled in?" she asked sarcastically.

I nodded. "More or less, I suppose."

"Must be nice."

"Why don't you grab your stuff and have a seat?"

"Nah, I'm good."

"Oh, please. The room back there's like a broom closet. No one can function like that, all cramped together like sardines. Just work in here."

"Manager won't be happy."

I shrugged. "That's her problem."

"Sure, except you won't get bitched at. I will."

"You won't."

She hesitated for a few seconds, then stepped out and returned with her backpack and another chair. She took a seat across from me with a look of impending doom on her face.

No sooner had she done that than a white SUV pulled into the parking lot. Cars of that size were quite the rarity in

Japan. A heavyset woman in a puffy white coat climbed out and bounded towards the school.

"Here we go," Silvia muttered.

Manager walked in and went straight for the break room, not noticing the two of us to her right. There was some quick chatter from back where the JTs were working, which quickly escalated in volume as one dominant voice tore into the others. It abruptly stopped and the sound of heavy footfalls rumbled in our direction.

She hadn't yet taken off her coat as she stood in the doorway, her sizable bulk filling the frame in its entirety. A trace of ire lingered on her face before vanishing into a smile of agonizing plasticity that rivaled even my own. I stood to greet her. Silvia sat motionless, her back towards the door and staring at the wall.

"*Ohayo gozaimasu!*" I announced with a bow.

"Welcome, Matt sensei!" she replied. "Did you find the school okay this morning?"

"I did! Silvia here showed me the way."

"Oh, well, we all love Silvia," she answered with a quick glance at the back of Silvia's head. "And you got your schedule?"

"Right here," I said, holding up the paper. "Haruna gave it to me. I hope it's okay that I'm working in here. I need a lot of space since I'm so tall."

"Oh, no, that's totally fine!" she giggled.

"And I asked Silvia to help me with a bunch of things, too. I feel bad for taking up so much of her time, but she's been very patient with me. The folks in Okayama will be happy to hear how great she's been."

Her smile faded and she nodded thoughtfully. "Well, you

two can use this room whenever you want. And I'm always available if you need anything!"

"Thank you, Manager!" I said as I sat down again. She turned and was gone.

Silvia was beaming like I'd just slain a dragon, her mouth gaping in an incredulous grin from ear to ear. Her eyes met mine for the first time.

"So, where are you from?" I asked.

It's amazing how people change when the pressure drops. Having enough space to work was such a potent release valve that Silvia was a different human being by the end of the week. It was like meeting her all over again, and the new her suited me just fine. It was a good thing, too – the brutality of the winter was killing everyone's attitude. There was a cloud of grumpiness floating around that I couldn't brush away no matter how cheerful I acted. The energy in my classes was at an all-time low. The teachers weren't spared, either. Manager continued her abuse of the JTs (though never when I was present) and I spotted Haruna once or twice with tears in her eyes.

The start of 2004 was not a happy time. I was lucky to have someone to lean on.

Now that her shell was off, Silvia from Atlanta was cool as hell. She sported that good southern charm, drank whiskey by choice, and had *spectacular* taste in music. She'd pop over to my place at least twice a week after work (I had better speakers) and we'd savor some Johnny Walker Black on the way down the next rabbit hole in her vast .mp3 collection. She'd been downloading music like a fiend the entire four months she'd been in Japan. Some of my own most treasured albums to this day came from the vault of that Georgia peach.

We were listening to one of our mutual drum 'n' bass heroes one evening when her eyes suddenly went wider than dinner plates. She looked like she'd seen a ghost.

"Rolling papers?" she whispered.

I looked over my shoulder. There they were, sitting on top of the bookcase for the whole world to see. I was stupefied by my own carelessness. "Uhhh... maybe?"

She lurched forward and grabbed my hand, squeezing it with the force of a dozen men. "Please tell me you've got weed."

Crisis averted. "Affirmative," I replied.

She let go of my hand and hers went to her mouth. "Can we smoke?" she squeaked. It was the most imploring voice anyone had ever used on me.

"But of course!" I smiled. I reached over to the top drawer, pulled out the chubby little bag of grass and tossed it to her.

She turned it over in her hand as if it were the Hope Diamond. "Where the hell did you get this?"

"My buddy Glenn in Kumagaya has a hookup. You should meet Glenn, you'd like him. Big into house music."

"Yeah? Is he cute?"

"Oh, God, no. You wanna roll, or should I?"

"I'll do it," Silvia said. "It's been way too long."

I handed her the papers and watched her work. She was clearly no stranger to the task and completed it with skilled hands and impressive speed. I stood up and went over to shut the curtains. Old habits.

"No, don't do that," Silvia said with surprising force. "I hate closed curtains, too claustrophobic. Curtains should only be closed when you're doing something that's illegal to do in public."

I acquiesced and sat back down. "And this doesn't qualify?"

"Nah," she muttered through the doobie hanging from her lips. "Lighter?"


I mentioned to Silvia one stony evening that meditation was part of my nightly routine.

"Wait here," she blurted out suddenly, and ran out the front door. A minute later she reappeared, carrying a single jewel case with a burnt CD inside. Without another word she collapsed in front of my laptop and had it queued up. "You ready for this?"

I nodded.

She then unleashed a blazing intergalactic pulsar of musical divinity that struck me stupid from the very first chord. I reeled as the breath leapt from my body – it was like someone had reached into my soul and strummed it like a harp. The two of us lay on the floor in silence, drinking it in the way you're supposed to. Every now and then Silvia's arm reached out to the air and waved with the melody as if conducting an invisible celestial orchestra. By the time the album peaked in the sixth track I was practically weeping. I picked up the jewel case and looked at the cover. On an undeserving scrap of paper taped to the front were six words written in blue sharpie. I read them out loud.

"Chill in India by Alex Seoan."

KURASHIKI WINTER SICKNESS

"Damn right," Silvia's voice answered.

"Jesus Lord, who is this guy?"

"No idea," she said. "He's from South America, I think. I don't even remember where I found this."

"Burn me a copy?"

"You can have that one."

Talk about the gift that kept on giving. I've meditated to that album countless times since that night. Even now it remains my go-to device for slipping the bonds of this corporeal existence to spend a few blissful moments in auditory nirvana.

We listened to the last three tracks in silence, each of us lost in whatever universe we'd drifted off to. Finally it stopped and we just lay there looking at the ceiling, basking in the residual afterglow of that extraordinary stretch of music.

"I hate it here."

I blinked hard and snapped back to reality. Did she say that or had I just imagined it?

"What?"

"I hate it here," Silvia repeated. "Not *here* here, like with you. I hate Japan. I need to get out of here."

Was she serious? Nobody hated Japan.

"You've seen how it is at work," she went on. "Manager's a cunt. She's made me feel unwelcome since day one. She didn't even meet me at the station when I arrived or show me around or anything. Not one word of encouragement from her, ever. It's so constantly toxic at the school that everyone just wants to get the hell out of there. None of the JTs ever get together outside of work, so I've barely even met anyone. I have zero Japanese friends.

Haruna's okay, but she's constantly with her boyfriend and never around. I've barely even seen the town. I hardly ever go out to the clubs or the bars or do anything fun. On the weekends I just want to sleep."

"I didn't really have any Japanese friends in Nagaoka, either," I confessed. "I never had the energy to go out and make any."

"Right?" Silvia said. "How are we supposed to even learn Japanese if we're brainless from being worked half to death? This idea that you can just pick up the language by living somewhere is total bullshit."

I nodded. "Yeah, it is. I've been completely disabused of that myth."

"It sucks. My life sucks here. I go to work, I come home. I go to work, I come home. I'm by myself all the time, just sitting on my ass in my apartment."

"I know the feeling," I replied.

A heavy silence lingered before she spoke again. "I just miss my family," she sighed.

There it was. "Classic homesickness," I told her. "So, you're human."

She rolled over to the laptop to find a new album. "Well, screw it," she said with a clap of her hands as the music started up again. "I'm home in thirteen days."

I flipped through the calendar in my head. There were no holidays coming up. "Why are you going home?"

She clicked her tongue. "'Cause I quit."

"You quit?!"

"Yep. I told Manager I was breaking my contract and gave her a 30-day notice."

"Oh, man," I groaned. "When was this?"

"I dunno. A few days before you got here?" she answered, lying back down again. "The look on that bitch's face was priceless."

"Are you for real?" I blurted out. "When were you gonna tell me?" Something irked me about how casually she was telling me all this.

"I barely know you, honey," she said with a dry kind of laugh. "I don't have to tell you a thing."

I couldn't deny it – she was absolutely right. She didn't owe me an explanation. Who the hell was I, anyway? I suddenly felt like an ass for reacting like that.

"Wow," I sighed.

"Are you mad?"

"No, just bummed out. You were like the only thing that made this town bearable. But you're right, you don't owe me a thing. You can do whatever you want."

"So can you."

I was eager to change the subject. "So, what DO you do when you're just sitting on your ass in your apartment?"

She pushed herself up to her elbows and looked at her feet, tapping her toes together in time with the music. Maybe I'd pissed her off and she was ignoring me.

"Boring stuff," she answered when the song ended. "Read a lot of books, cook a lot of food. Watch a lot of porn."

An insipid chuckle burst from my teeth before I could stop it. "A lot of *porn*?"

"Tons of it." She glared at me with hard, wide eyes that drilled holes into mine.

I sat up, praying my voice wouldn't crack. "Are you trying to tell me something?"

"Maybe."

"Silvia, dear, I do believe you're baiting me."

"Maybe." She wasn't smiling now. "I really need to get fucked."

pregnancy! herpes! the clap! ...latex?

*Check. We are cleared for take-off.*

"Well," I shrugged, looking around at the empty apartment to make sure the coast was clear. "Here we are."

Her mouth curved into a wicked smile as she sprung up to draw the curtains.

LUNA decided that there weren't enough classes to justify a second FT, so Silvia had no replacement when she left. Everyone else at the school stayed unhappy and classes were a grind. The snow had stopped falling and was now amassed on every street corner in filthy, gray heaps. The whole town was swallowed up by an aura of desolation. I was itching to move on, though I still had no news about my next assignment. The suspense was murder.

"Who knows?" I said to Silvia as the cab driver loaded her bags. "You may remember this place with more fondness than you think."

"Anything's possible," she shrugged. I didn't know her well enough to read her expression, but I knew a forced smile when I saw one.

I handed her a scrap of paper with my email address on it. "Don't be a stranger," I said. "Drop me a line from time to time, okay?"

"I will," she said. She climbed into the back seat and was gone.

she won't.

*No, she won't. Ships in the night.*

The call came three days before I was set to leave. My next stint would be a long one. I would be replacing Janet, the outgoing teacher at one of the three schools in Hiroshima.

Yes, THAT Hiroshima.

# TRANSCENDING HIROSHIMA

The name was infamous, of course. Anyone who's spent five minutes in a U.S. History class knows about Hiroshima, and for exactly one reason. I'd heard the story often, particularly since my dad, like many of his generation, was enamored with WWII and had a kind of macabre reverence for its grand finale. The idea of living in that city was just bizarre. The idea of *anyone* still living in that city was just bizarre. It had been synonymous with death and destruction since before I was born, only existing in my mind as a kind of ghost town. My new home.

It was a two-hour train ride west from Kurashiki. The unfamiliar landscape of Western Japan glided by my window, the Shinkansen again proving itself the finest apparatus of public transportation ever conceived. Why they can't manage to replicate it in America still baffles me.

The train turned into a taxi. We crossed four bridges between the airport and Koi, the neighborhood in greater Hiroshima where I'd be living. Bright lights, neon signs, restaurants, stores, hotels, gas stations, parks, arcades, and a crap-ton of people decorated the city like anywhere else. Nothing about it matched the weirdness I felt about being there. We even found ourselves in a traffic jam. Wonder of wonders! You mean this is actually a living, breathing community of human beings?

of course it is, you dumbass.

*Shut up.*

I shook my head and finally relaxed in my seat. How idiotic I was to hold a 1945-centric view of what was now a thriving, modern metropolis of over a million people. And what a delightful change to be in the big city! The buildings got taller and taller as we crept through a maze of busy intersections and traffic lights, then vanished abruptly as we approached another bridge. The noise from the crowd outside swelled to a roar.

"*Are wa nan desu ka?*" *(What is that?)* I asked the taxi driver in my busted Japanese.

"Baseball game!" he replied in comparable English, pointing to the right. Across the street loomed a monstrous stadium, shattering the night with white lights and the cheers of thousands of fans of the Hiroshima Carps. A game was in full swing (an odd thing in February), and a four-block stomping ground surged with the blissful energy of the great American pastime. A twinge of patriotic pride went through me as I saw my country's most boring export bringing joy to so many. At that moment, I was darn proud to be from the good ol' U.S. of A.

Then I looked to my left.

The lights of the city died, replaced by a dim, ominous glow that shimmered green along the riverbank. Silhouettes of trees appeared in no discernible pattern around a solitary, ruined structure that stood at the edge of the water, gazing lifelessly at its own reflection. I knew this building from pictures in Lonely Planet – the A-Bomb Dome – the only structure of the old city that had survived the cataclysm. The joy of baseball was instantly erased.

"Where are you from?" the driver suddenly asked, smiling.

"Canada," I replied.


Another absurdly large apartment. Unlike the one I inhabited in Kurashiki, however, the living area was tiny. All the excessive space was in the kitchen, which didn't help me at all. What the hell was I going to do with a gigantic kitchen? Dinner parties? It wasn't even a nice one – the cabinets were old and crooked, the paint was a ghastly shade of maroon, and there were nails sticking out of the walls in at least three places.

I lost myself to a mental temper-tantrum before I remembered I didn't care. These were the trivialities I constantly made too big a deal of. I quit my bitching and paid no more heed to the sorry state of the place.

*What about the next teacher?*

Good point. I had to consider the next poor soul who'd be stuck here. What if I'd walked into an apartment like this on that first day in Nagaoka? It's hard enough picking up and moving to a foreign country, starting a new job, and adjusting to a new life. Throw a run-down home into that mix and you've got a big problem. If the next foreign teacher had to deal with that, odds are they'd bail early and another ET would be sent right back again.

I called up Brian in Okayama and told him the deal.

"Write a letter," he said. "Describe everything wrong with the place and mail it to me here at HQ right away."

I sat down on the floor of my freakishly wide kitchen, filled with a new and benevolent mission to save my successor from misery. I scrapped my plans for the day and started writing, then began my mythical quest for the post office.

Janet, my predecessor, had left a bike in the garage and a sticky note on the fridge describing what it looked like. Description or not, picking an unfamiliar bicycle out of a lineup was not easy. They all looked the same to me. Plus, everyone and their brother has at least one, so every bike rack is jam packed throughout the day. A buffet of profanities was served to the chilly morning air before I finally found it.

The quest was achieved when I came across the post office three blocks away and mailed the letter. I then turned my bike towards downtown, taken by a sudden desire for a closer look at the A-Bomb Dome. All I had to do was follow the main road over three (or was it four?) bridges and it would eventually appear on the right. I couldn't possibly miss the humungous stadium right across from it, could I?

The A-Bomb Dome lies at the edge of what is now the "Peace Park," a vast public space built upon the remains of ground zero as a memorial to the victims of war, and a reminder of the horror of nuclear weapons. It starts (or ends) at the river about fifty feet from the side of the road, unmissable from the bridge that approaches it. The dome stands there timidly, dwarfed by the taller office buildings and apartment complexes surrounding the park, as if trying not to be noticed. It might be easy for an outsider to overlook but for the bewilderment it engenders. Why would a burnt-out corpse of a building occupy such a prime piece of real estate in the heart of the city? Why haven't they torn it down and replaced it with cheaply-made, overpriced condos?

I rode the brake down the gentle decline of the bridge, turning right onto a footpath that ran along the edge of the river and coming to a stop directly in front of what was once the front door.

The building towered over me, menacing and cold. Strewn about its base lay broken slabs of concrete that had once comprised its façade, while the charred outer walls had been partially reconstructed to show their original outline. What remained of the internal structure was a scarred patchwork of black, white, and red brick that gave the impression of burnt human flesh. It was crowned by the rusted skeleton of a metal dome that miraculously avoided collapse, giving the building its name. Peering through any of the hollow doorways or windows offered a view straight through to the trees on the other side. The interior had been utterly disemboweled by hellfire. No one inside stood a chance that day.

*It happened right here.* In the sky above where I stood,

mankind's ultimate weapon was unleashed upon the earth. A nuclear explosion, directly over my head. Standing there gave me the creeps.

What inconceivable madness – how could it have ever come to this? Play the blame game with WWII until you're blue in the face. There were a hundred thousand people vaporized, burned alive, or poisoned to death that day who had nothing to do with it.

Neither did I, of course. The guilt still lingered.


My classroom looked like it had recently played host to a pack of coked-up velociraptors. Half-shredded posters hung from the walls, textbooks were bent and squeezed into a single, minuscule bookcase in no conceivable order, the alphabet sign was missing letters, the CD player looked like it was itching to electrocute someone, and the window was covered in faded, ancient-looking stickers, thwarting any natural light that might have been. The centerpiece of it all, however, was the small mountain of garbage amassed in the far corner, taking up a fifth of the room's floorspace. A student could easily dive in and make a trash angel. How could anyone function like this? This Janet person clearly had no control over her classroom.

what a slob.

Hey, don't judge.

Once the initial shock had worn off, I began to consider her plight. You have to be really miserable to walk away from a gig like teaching in Japan. Silvia's case was simple – an abusive boss is more than enough to drive someone away. But the manager here in Koi was a delight from what I could tell. So, what did Janet in? Was it a hundred little things or something more traumatic? Did she have no one like Glenn or Celine to lean on when things got dark? Would she always remember her brief time in Japan as a failure? Standing there amidst the mess I imagined all sorts of depressing scenarios. Poor kid. I hope everything worked out for her.

Oh, well, there was nothing for it. My place was in the here and now. I walked back to the lobby, told the manager I needed three hours and two plastic trash bags, and went to work. I made that room tidier than an army barracks. By lunchtime the walls were clean, the windows clear, and Garbage Mountain was no more. I even made some new games to drive home the "out with the old, in with the new" feeling about the place.

The manager and the other JTs were astonished by the change. Evidently, this particular classroom had been an embarrassment – a stain on an otherwise respectable facility – but the staff had always been too timid to mention it. That was probably part of the problem. In any case, the gratitude displayed was downright celebratory, elevating me to hero status. They really made too big a deal out of it. I just didn't want to work on top of a landfill.

My Koi students were the best and brightest I'd had in Japan. Either I was a more effective teacher by then or these kids were just better behaved in general (or both), but something about the dynamic in that school made teaching a breeze. Maybe the children appreciated having a classroom that wasn't a disaster zone. There was also the theory that city kids had an entirely different vibe than rural kids as a result of their environment, and this somehow made them more personable. Though counter-intuitive to me, this was a hypothesis staunchly held by Celine.

"Hey, loser!" she shouted over the phone two weeks later. "Guess where they're sending me next?"

"Neptune?"

"Ha, ha. I'll give you a hint... you'll be able to buy me dinner!"


Celine arrived in Hiroshima the following Sunday. The FT from the LUNA school downtown had bowed out for reasons unknown and my partner-in-crime was tapped as the replacement. How's that for serendipity? The two of us hung out whenever it was warm enough to be outside, exploding fireworks by the river (totally legal) and partaking in our cherished, weekend ritual of "freak watching" while day-drinking lime daiquiris in the city center.

What freaks, you ask? Well, at this moment in Japanese history the phenomenon of *ganguro* (extreme tanning) was raging, reaching peak insanity around the time of my arrival. It was a fad propagated by a magazine I'll call "Nog" (true name not disclosed here), wherein teenage girls would tan themselves to a crisp, bleach their hair, and wear what amounted to clown makeup. We could spot them in a crowd from a hundred yards away since they always traveled in packs and were 200% louder than anyone in the vicinity.

From head to toe they were utterly unnatural, the living representation of a fashion craze gone off the rails. So, Celine and I considered it good clean fun to post up, get

THE SAGE AND THE GREMLIN

toasted, and make fun of them as they passed by.

Celine's manager, Kumiko, occasionally invited us over to her house in the burbs to have dinner with the folks from the third (and largest) LUNA school in Hiroshima. There were two FTs at that one, Patricia and Maya, from Charlotte and Vancouver, respectively. We met each other on Kumiko's balcony – a massive open-air platform overlooking the entire city and littered with some truly righteous toys. Her kids had amassed quite a collection of samurai swords and other plastic weaponry. Celine and I started battling with them immediately, much to the indignation of their owners.

Patricia was nice enough but perpetually distant, as if never really enjoying herself. Her smile and her politeness were kind but forced. She was dealing with a long-distance relationship in a state of decline and was counting the unhappy days until her contract was up and she could get back to her life stateside.

Maya was a gem. She was relentlessly optimistic about life and had a way of making everyone around her feel better about themselves. She and Patricia had become besties in no time, as she too was in a committed, Trans-Pacific relationship and could empathize with Patricia's plight. She was a listener, and did it well. And do forgive me, she was a knockout to the -nth degree. I couldn't help but compare her to the long-lost Chantelle, though Maya struck me as warmer, more reserved and less abrasive. Her biggest problem, Celine and I soon discovered, was that she felt personally responsible for Patricia's happiness and spent nearly all her free time trying to cheer her up. It was a futile endeavor and her social life paid the price. Unless she was having acute boyfriend problems herself and needed to blow off steam with a night on the town, Maya was nearly always MIA.

She also didn't get how Celine and I could be so close without our relationship ever going hot. She just assumed the two of us were an item from the way we acted. Her misconceptions were understandable, as I explained on one of the rare occasions I was able to coax her out to the pubs. Celine and I just weren't each other's type.

"So what *is* your type?" she asked me through a mouthful of martini olives.

"Oh, you know. Dark hair, pretty eyes. Loves olives."

oh, for god's sake.

*Still got it!*

She rolled her eyes with a snort, but was still smiling. "Such a smoothie. You know I have a boyfriend, right?"

"Yeah, you may have mentioned it once or twice."

The phone rang early Sunday morning. It was Brian.

"Pack your bags," he told me. "We're getting you out of that apartment *today*. Your manager will meet you at the school at 9:00 a.m. and take you over to your new place."

I was packed and out the door without so much as a last look at the place, bounding out of the building and across the street to the river. Something about the air smelled different this morning. Better. I took a deep breath, conjured the good ol' orb, and started walking, elated by this sudden move towards the unknown, even if it was just for a few blocks. What would my new apartment be like?

It was a straight shot along the river for ten minutes, with only one turn onto the street where the school was located. I arrived a few minutes early and no one was there to meet me. Whatever, there was a Lawson at the end of the street. I popped in for a quick breakfast of coffee and *o-nigiri*, which was this delightful triangular snack of rice, tuna, and seaweed. There were variations, of course, but the tuna was always my go-to. To keep the seaweed crispy, *o-nigiri* was packaged in a way that required a three-stage unwrapping process done in the correct sequence with just the right amount of force. One wrong move and the whole thing fell apart in your hands. I'd ruined dozens of them.

Celine was always up at this hour for her morning walk, so I gave her a call. No answer. I tried Glenn, but there was no way in hell he was up this early. He was probably just leaving the clubs now, God bless him. No answer there, either. It was just as well, as Manager turned the corner as I hung up. I jumped to my feet, thrilled at the idea of riding in a car (a rare occurrence), and brought my suitcase over to the trunk.

"No, no," Manager blurted out. "We're only going upstairs."

Okay, that was weird. At least, it would have been at any other time – my definition of weirdness had long since grown to encompass only the truly, unequivocally bizarre. But now I was even more curious. I'd never even considered the mysterious floors above the school at ground level. Heck, I hadn't even noticed that other door to the left of the entrance. We stepped through it, into an elevator and

Manager pushed three. Seven seconds later the doors opened again. We walked to the end of the hall, stopping in front of a door sporting a shiny chrome "303". Then it hit me – this was a residential building. These were apartments. This was *my* apartment!

proximity alert! they want you to live at the school! they want to chain you to your desk! they —

*Quiet!*

The damage was done – the Gremlin had stabbed my mind with a splinter of dread. It took thirty seconds to get from my place of business to my new fortress of solitude. *Thirty seconds.* That was no distance at all. There was no buffer, no demilitarized zone between the two blood enemies of work and home. The last thing I wanted was for someone, *anyone* from the school to ever come knocking on my front door. That would be an earth-shattering collision of personal and professional worlds, and it only had to happen once to annihilate any sense of sanctuary. But there was nothing to be done – I'd brought this on myself complaining about the last place. Time to reap what I'd sewn.

"What do you think?" Manager smiled.

"It looks great, thank you!" The words were sticky in my mouth.

My new lair was smaller than the last one, but more optimized to make use of the space it had. It was also younger – clean wooden counters and shiny metal surfaces in the kitchen, smooth, neutral-colored wallpaper, perfectly level floors, and spotless wall-to-wall carpet in the living area. It even had that "new apartment" smell to it. My dread subsided, and after a week or so without incident I realized my fears were baseless – no one from work was ever coming uninvited to my home. They knew better than that.

Having the school right downstairs had its perks. I could zip back to my apartment every day during my lunch hour. I'd fling off my work clothes, gobble down whatever I had lying around, and spend the rest of the hour meditating, returning to work 59 minutes later thoroughly rejuvenated and ready to crush the rest of my day. It was the greatest work-life balance I'd ever achieved.

*And you were worried, silly boy.*


It happened on a Saturday.

I was up later than usual, beginning my evening ritual around 11:00 p.m. It started like any other – a candle burned faintly in the dark, illuminating the gold-painted happy Buddha I'd bought myself as a housewarming present. The only other light was the blue power indicator on my computer, which was easy to ignore. Alex Hephaestion's *Ambient Nights: Brighton Beach* (get this album) had become my latest addiction and played at a pleasant volume through the laptop's external speakers behind me.

An uninterrupted, two-week stretch of nightly meditation had made life better all around. All my little aches and pains had vanished from the stretching, I was sleeping more soundly than ever, and my confidence was sky high. Best of all, the Gremlin was fading. It still landed a punch from time to time, but the Sage was winning the fight.

I sat on the floor in the half-lotus, breathing in the subtle, splendid aroma of the *nag champa* burning in the corner. My head drifted forward as if I were about to nod off. The Buddha glided upwards in my field of vision as my eyes dropped down. The music was suddenly different, distant somehow, as if I were only hearing its echo. Out of nowhere came the sensation of falling backwards and upwards, as if I were submerged in breathable water and a buoyant force was gently pushing me up to the surface while my body remained just a few inches below.

Then it got weird. The world before me abruptly lost its three-dimensionality, appearing instead as a flat canvas that at once enveloped me, the room, and everything, *everything* behind me, in time and in space. All the knowledge on every subject I'd ever learned anything about leapt from my mind and imprinted itself on the canvas, as if the entire history of human civilization was placed in front of me like some fifth grader's diorama. My individual distinctiveness vanished, replaced by an undeniable sense of oneness with all creation. And yet I sensed nothing spiritual or supernatural at work. It felt scientific, more a discovery than a revelation, bombarding me with conclusions I'd long suspected to be true. The singular nature of the universe became overwhelmingly apparent, *stupidly* obvious in those moments, and I was as inseparable from it as a drop of water in an ocean. And the ocean stretched to infinity in every direction. What followed was an injection of emotion directly to the heart, *Pulp Fiction*-style. I vaguely recall splashes of terror, anguish, and euphoric joy. But they were too brief to really register in my conscious mind. It was like suddenly waking up from a dream in which someone throws a bucket of ice water at you.

Then it was over.

My body shuddered as I gasped, snapping me out of my meditative state. The world was its boring old 3D self again, my cozy Hiroshima apartment back to its normal form and function. The shock lingered as I caught my breath, a severe case of pins and needles fluttering across my skin. And, of course, a monumental sense of *what... the... fuck.*

No drugs.


There was no way I was going to trust my lousy memory to be the sole record keeper of what just happened. I rolled out of the futon over to where my laptop sat on the *kutatsu* (a little table with a heater), threw open the lid and double-clicked on Notepad. After a minute looking at a blank screen, terrified of forgetting, I forced myself to type something. Anything. Just type, you stupid bastard, before it's gone. Slowly my fingers began to move.

it was like...
blinking. out of existence and into... something else.
what, though? everything that's me evaporates, vanishes
to infinity. a raindrop falling to earth and colliding with
an invisible ocean. ocean of dreams? quiet, swirling sea
of everything before and after. fluid. a clean, warm bath.
so, so welcome. no fear. i'm gone, blasted outwards... a
revelation, a nova... subatomic and sublime. microscopic
and telescopic, both directions. all directions. what was
it? fall into the world's deepest hole and land on the

world's biggest trampoline. ha! no stairway? a catapult to heaven! thrown out of myself and redistributed to everywhere. everything gone but nothing lost. nothing there but nothing missing. what was it? so welcome. no fear. darkness replaced by invisible light. no, that's not it. not darkness on one side and light on the other. not cancelling out the other. one and the same. swirling... both and neither all at once. existence and void. the is and the isn't, both one. unity. something singular, encompassing, everywhere. nowhere. complete but always beginning. forever and never. something else.

I re-read the text. Who was I, James Joyce on a bender? What a bunch of schlock. My hand smacked the lid and the laptop clapped shut. I stepped out onto the balcony, taken by a sudden urge to be outside. The hills at the edge of town were great black shadows hidden by the dark of night. I tried describing the "something else" to myself out loud, but that wasn't any easier than trying to write it. All I did was compare it to some concept or object I already knew, all of which were small, earthly things. I tried again and again, thwarted by the limitations of my feeble little language. This thing I'd stumbled across could barely be conceptualized in my own brain, so how the hell could I ever explain it? It was like...

Then something clicked.

Goosebumps danced up and down my torso as I lurched back inside. "Shit, where'd I put it?" I asked the rug. I spun towards the corner, toes slamming into the laptop I'd left on the floor. I skidded it away with my foot, threw open the closet door and pulled out my trusty olive-green backpack.

It still reeked of India tourist perfume – sunblock, sweat, bug spray, and incense. I rummaged through the junk at the bottom, my fingers finally closing around a familiar flat object. The backpack fell to the floor again as I flipped open the abused paperback and read the very first line:

*"The Tao that can be spoken is not the true Tao."*

I fell to the couch and read the next page.

*"Being and non-being create each other."*

By the end of page three I could barely breathe.

*"Practice not doing, and everything falls into place."*

I read the *Tao Te Ching* in two hours. How could I not? Here was this old Chinese guy from Greco-Roman times describing, in detail, everything I'd experienced meditating over the past year. All that ethereal, next-level weirdness that went on in my thoughtless mind put into 81 bite-sized bits of prose. Here, a far more literate hand than my own had chronicled the journey – a revered voice from Antiquity reaching out through the millennia to let me know I wasn't crazy. This stuff was real. Hell, it was so real it became a way of life for millions of people in East Asia. A religion, even, though nothing about the text struck me as religious. There were no gods or angels, no reincarnations, rituals, or sacraments. It wasn't prophetic or proselytizing, and it said nothing about the afterlife. It was simply one man's account of achieving a state of enlightenment and the great mystery he found once he got there. A treatise on meditation directly from the mind of its greatest master. A call to the world for everyone to get over themselves and chill the fuck out, copyright 500 B.C.

That's how I took it, anyway.

So there it was, an explanation of the inexplicable. I read it over and over, instantly addicted. You know you've got a great book on your hands when you occasionally toss it across the room in amazement. Some verses I could read once and just think about for hours, while others struck chords so deep I could only hang my head and lament the follies of humanity. There were even a few that made no sense to me, but that was okay. I was only twenty-three. How much actual wisdom could I have accumulated in my trite little life thus far?

As a bonus, the yin-yang went from a slick surfer decal to a symbol of enormous significance. One side falling downwards into non-being, the other rising up from it, forming a perfect circle of existence in its purest form. It was a flawless visual representation of the meditative process. Learn to shut your mind all the way off and it will turn on again, brighter than ever, revealing its deepest, most powerful potential – to experience, as Lao named it, the *Tao*.

I tried to recreate the experience, of course. For several nights I sat in the same spot in the same position and listened to the same music as that night, hoping the memory of it might somehow trigger it again. Nope. It was self-defeating, like trying to force myself to forget something. Whatever it was, it wasn't coming back.

But something else lingered that wasn't there before – closure. A dull, barely perceptible sense of urgency for the next step, as if something had ended and something else was waiting to begin.

# LONG NIGHT ON THE MOUNTAIN

The ferry motor chugged like a locomotive as Celine and I made our way to Miyajima, one of the many islands off the southern coast of Hiroshima. Miyajima was the home of Mount Misen and the Itsukushima Shrine, a UNESCO World Heritage site and one of Japan's national treasures. We'd taken several weekend trips out there to "get more nature in our lives" as Celine put it. She listened with great interest as I told her about my so-called "moment of transcendence," responding only with "That is so cool!" at key points in the story. When I got to the part about the weird sense of closure I'd been feeling ever since, her smile vanished.

"Did you get your contract renewal for next year?" she suddenly asked. I hadn't. I hardly ever checked my mail. Why bother? It's not like I could read it. Any important news always came to me from Manager or from Okayama.

"No, you did?" I replied.

"Yep, I'm not staying. I'm done with Japan."

It took a second to absorb. The shock that buzzed through me just then had no rational explanation – of course she wasn't going to stay forever. Celine was the kind of person with a map of her whole life sketched out in her head, and Japan was only a variable in the equation. So why did my stomach just drop?

A minute went by as Miyajima slowly pulled towards the port bow. We stared at it in silence, listening to the roar of the ferry motor and the waves slapping against the hull. Then something came out of my mouth that surprised the hell out of me. Not the words themselves, but how strangely comfortable I was with saying them.

"Yeah, me too."

And with that, the countdown to the end of my excellent adventure began. Clouds once again enshrouded my future – I hadn't a clue what would come after Japan. Shouldn't I be worried?

"So, what are you gonna do next?" I asked Celine.

"Grad school in Paris," she replied, as if were the most boring thing in the world.

"Wait, *Paris?*" I blurted out. "When the hell did *this* happen?"

She leaned back on the rail, facing the deck again. "I decided a couple years ago. They've got one of the best diplomacy schools in the world there."

"And they accepted *you?*"

She ignored the dig. "Not yet, but they will."

"Wowww," I grinned. "You sure about that?"

"Of course I'm sure. I'm the shit."

There wasn't a trace of levity anywhere on her face, so I didn't push it. As the boat docked and we began to disembark, I turned to the next order of business.

"We're still doing Southeast Asia, right?" I called out as I followed Celine down the gangway. I already knew the answer.

"Fucking hell yes!" she bellowed.

Summer in Hiroshima was my happiest time in Japan. My students were fantastic, my boss and fellow teachers loved me, I was living in the perfect spot, and the weather was just how I like it. I even started running down by the river in the mornings, so my energy levels were at a record high. Glenn and his new girlfriend Natsumi accepted our invitation to join our quest to Southeast Asia, so we'd be rolling four deep. To top it all off, Patricia (remember Patricia?) packed up and left Japan during the first weekend of June, releasing Maya from her self-assigned duties as her personal therapist. With that shadow lifted, she was much more prone to going out in the evenings and we got to see a lot more of her.

It occurred to me one particularly warm and mellow evening as I was riding along the river that I'd stopped meditating over a week ago. The realization was so startling that I slammed the brakes and skidded to a halt. I couldn't believe it – my precious routine, neglected? Overlooked? Tossed aside like an old sock? Shame on me! I silently berated myself as I stared at the motionless water.

But the derision didn't last and curiosity took over. Why had I stopped? Why hadn't I noticed? And why, now that the shock had worn off, did I feel no pressure to start again?

I'd been practicing for so long that I was pretty good at it by now, surely. Maybe I no longer had to go down the ritual road of fire, music, floor, and orb to get to Meditation Town. Was I already there? Had I never left? Was it possible I'd been meditating without even realizing it? Had the line between a "meditative" state and a "normal" state of mind become somehow blurred?

The theory demanded immediate testing. I got back on my bike and rode to the arcade next to the Peace Park, which was always buzzing with people. I hopped off, walked into the middle of the crowd and just stood there. Then I subjected myself to the ultimate test – eye contact with an unfamiliar human being. Staring is an innately threatening behavior throughout the animal kingdom. We hairless apes are no exception.

Getting stared at by Japanese folks was part of my reality and had long ceased to bother me. But now I started staring back. I looked around until I met someone's eyes, then held their gaze. My first victim was a middle-aged man in a gray suit. My eyes fixed on his as my head turned to follow him. He immediately turned away and kept walking. I felt nothing. No trace of the familiar little electric pulse down my spine that eye contact had always delivered. I chose someone else. One of a pair of very loud teenage girls. Nada. An old woman with an umbrella. Another guy in a suit. Student after student after student, from grade school on up. Nothing. Not the slightest hint of unease or self-consciousness from something that should have been totally weird. Amazing. I stifled a victorious laugh and got back on my bike.

Still, this wasn't meditation, was it? I wasn't *trying* to clear my head or tune anything out, it was happening all by itself. Or was it not happening at all? Was I just different now? Could this be the lasting effect of such a consistent routine, some unconscious habit I'd formed that was now part of my personality? If so, it was a good one. It was like I'd spent months at the gym and was finally in decent shape, or I'd taken the last of my medicine and my body had managed to fight off the infection.

I felt *cured.*


July 4$^{th}$ is not nearly as fun outside the U.S., especially when your friends are Canadian. I nonetheless refused to let the day pass without at least some degree of celebration, however minor. Fortunately, neither Celine nor Maya needed convincing to take part. Maya never partied quite as hard as Celine and I, but she'd been winning our respect with distinguished acts of inebriate tomfoolery ever since Patricia left. Patricia's replacement, Vivian, was a proper grown-up with a whole family of her own, so we hardly ever saw her.

The three of us came across a pub by Carp Stadium that was owned by an old man who was absolutely in love with baseball. He'd thrown up a few American flags and wore a Chicago Cubs hat to mark the occasion. My heart glowed as we sat at the bar and I ordered a Sam Adams. In this kind of scenario, a little bit goes a long way.

"I have news!" Celine declared as we toasted our glasses.

"You made bail?" I quipped. Maya snorted a laugh.

"No, but did you know there's a jail like half a mile from my apartment?"

Maya gasped. "Whaaaat?"

"Yep," Celine nodded. "I've passed by it like a hundred times and always thought it was a high school or something."

I shrugged. "Same thing."

"Ha!" Celine laughed. "Jail, high school, whatever!"

Maya was examining some wasabi peanuts. "You didn't like high school, huh?"

"Hated it," I said. "Don't even get me started."

Celine's eyes widened. "Really? I loved high school! It was super easy and we just partied all the time."

"I never partied," I lamented. "Not cool enough."

"So, tell us your news!" Maya said with a nudge to Celine.

"Oh yeah! LUNA found my replacement so I'm leaving Hiroshima."

I crushed a coaster in my hand. "No! Boo!"

"Wow, that was fast," Maya said with a wince. She'd popped one of the peanuts in her mouth and regretted it immediately.

"I know, it kinda sucks," Celine replied. "But that's not the good part. Guess where I'm going next?"

"Tokyo?"

"Okinawa?"

"Nope," Celine beamed. "Nagaoka!"

I couldn't believe it. "No, you're not."

"Yep! Apparently the teacher who replaced you was a total weirdo and no one could stand him. Then one day he just showed up, told them he quit, and walked out. Real professional."

"Nagaoka was my first school," I explained to Maya. "Sounds like it's gone to the dogs."

THE SAGE AND THE GREMLIN

Celine smiled. "I'll whip that place into shape in no time. Plus, I get to work with your old Manager! She's gonna tell me all the embarrassing stories about you and we're gonna laugh and laugh and laugh!"

Maya shook her head. "You're so mean."

"No, no," I assured her. "This is Celine's way of showing affection. Deep down she's weeping over how much she'll miss me. And who can blame her?"

Maya flicked a peanut across the table at me. "What an ego! I can't believe you're leaving me here with this guy, Celine."

I clicked my tongue in feigned offense. "*Now* who's being mean?"

"Oh, you know I'm kidding."

"I'll definitely miss Hiroshima," Celine said. "I wish I could spend the rest of the summer here. This city is amazing."

"No doubt."

"Oh, well," she went on. "You two will just have to try to have fun without me."

A week later she was gone again. Much as I loved having Celine around, that particular goodbye was a breeze. We had an epic vacation to look forward to in September, after all.


*Obon* is a Japanese national holiday centered around a centuries-old Buddhist festival celebrating one's ancestors. For us *gai-jin* it meant a week off in mid-August. It was the last big holiday before I'd leave Japan, and I still hadn't climbed Mount Fuji. Unacceptable.

Glenn was of similar mind. He proposed a night out in

the capital to kick off *Obon*, then a day to re-charge the batteries back in Kumagaya before heading out to conquer the mountain. Natsumi had never climbed it, so she was in, too. Maya hadn't yet been to Tokyo, so I talked her into joining us for the first part of the plan. Mount Fuji wasn't on her bucket list, though, so she was heading back to Hiroshima after our business in the capital was concluded. Gigantic volcanoes aren't for everyone.

DJ Yoji, one of our local favorites, was scheduled to do a late-night set at Liquid Room, the same club where Glenn and I had our minds blown on our first trip to Tokyo. The four of us hung out at the bar getting toasted and shouting conversation while we waited for him to show up. Maya would sporadically drag me onto the dance floor to get down to one of her Top 40 favorites. I wasn't about to say no – she was positively radiating urban club girl hotness.

anyone ever tell you that you suck at dancing?

*Nonsense! We've got rhythm AND soul, bitch.*

Midnight came and the venue was still only half full, which was strange given Yoji's popularity at the time. Glenn and I watched the bartender assemble our second Jäger bomb of the evening as the girls danced the night away. Then he told me.

"So, I didn't renew for next year."

My eyes went wide. "For real? I thought you loved it here!"

"I do, man! I dig Japan. I just can't handle teaching anymore. It's not what I wanna do."

I couldn't argue with that. "So what's the plan? Head back to Arizona?"

"Dunno yet."

"What'll happen with you and Nat?"

"Dunno that either. We were talking about maybe her coming with me, but she's got a job and her family is all here, you know? We've got a buncha stuff we need to work out."

The lights turned up and the music abruptly changed to J-pop. A girl about our age appeared from behind the DJ booth, walked through the crowd and placed a single folding chair in the center of the dance floor. Maya and Nat slowly backed away and re-joined us at the bar.

"Is this some sort of break-dancing thing?" I yelled at Glenn.

"I don't think so, man…"

A younger girl sat down in the chair. The music continued with a horrid tune by Ayumi Hamasaki, the early 2000s Japanese equivalent of Britney Spears. Then, as if completely normal, the first girl came back to where the other was sitting, threw a barber cape over her, and proceeded to give her a haircut.

The four of us stood transfixed, waiting for the punchline of what could only be an elaborate joke of some sort. But it never came. This haircut was going to continue until it was good and done.

Now, for some people, a 1:00 a.m. trim in the middle of a crowded Tokyo nightclub while blasting obnoxious pop music might be normal. We *gai-jin* just weren't with the program. The girls fell over each other laughing while Glenn and I, disappointed that we would not be raging with Yoji that evening, took a bit longer to process the hilarity of the moment. We were out the door by 1:30 – early for a night out in Tokyo – and wandered back to the train station in silence, bitten by a chill in the air that none of us had expected. Yoji's non-appearance remains a mystery to this day.

The open-air platform blocked the wind just enough for us to feel human again. After Nat had nodded off on the train back to Kumagaya, I was able to pry some information out of Glenn – they still hadn't bought their tickets to Thailand. As I pressed upon him the urgency of getting them ASAP, his muted response left little doubt in my mind that they'd flake out. It was a gut-punch, but it was hardly something to give them shit about. If it was an issue of money (which I suspected) I didn't want to harp on it like an entitled douche. The frugal life in Nagaoka had left me with a respectable cash reserve, but that was me. I took a seat next to Maya, who was peering half-asleep out the window.

"Sure you don't want to come?" I asked her. I'd extended the invitation weeks before, but she hadn't amassed enough vacation time to make it happen.

Her face hardened. "Of course I *want* to come. You know I can't."

"Sure, you can. Just quit your job and start a new life in Bangkok. I bet English teachers make a killing over there!"

"Right. I'll do that." She closed her eyes and rested her head on the glass.

The train rolled by uneventfully, stopping along the way to let the night crawlers disembark.

I'm not sure what made me do it, but all of a sudden I looked over at the train map, written entirely in unintelligible Japanese. When we reached the next stop, the terrible truth occurred to me.

"We have to get off here!" I shouted, pulling Maya up by the arm and making for the open doors. Nat's eyes popped open. Glenn grabbed her by the hand and they followed me out as the doors shut again. In response to their perturbed looks I explained why I'd just lost my damn mind – we'd been going in the wrong direction the entire time.

Nat looked up at the map and slapped her forehead.

"Oh wow," Maya laughed. "We *are* idiots, aren't we?"

"Whoops," Glenn muttered.

We walked over to the other side of the platform to catch the train back in the right direction, feeling very, very stupid. But it was still pretty funny.

We waited 5...10...25 minutes. Nothing. A delay like this in Japan was unheard of. By now it was pushing 2:30 a.m. and we knew we'd missed the last train of the night. There wasn't a soul around, we had no ride, and the temperature was going nowhere but down.

Not funny.

Phone already at the ear, Nat was hopping from one foot to the next as we waited for her to pull a rabbit from her hat. Then she dropped her hand and swore loudly in Japanese.

"It died."

Several minutes of quiet, panicked brainstorming followed. We couldn't call a taxi because no one had a number for one, we couldn't walk anywhere because we didn't know the area, and we couldn't take a train because the damn things weren't running. So what now, call a coworker for advice? To hell with that. Sleep on the street? No, thank you, once was enough.

"Fuck it, he'll understand," Glenn finally said.

He walked a few steps away from me and Maya (who had stolen my hat and gloves) and made a call. With a tone apologetic enough to get a man off Death Row, he explained the situation to the person on the other end and asked the unthinkable – a ride for four from wherever the hell we were all the way back to Kumagaya. He fell silent on the line for a moment, then bounded over to the metro map outside the station and took a picture of it with his phone. A deafening silence passed as the rest of us looked on helplessly.

"Yes!" Glenn screamed at the mouthpiece. "Thank you so much, dude, you are my HERO! *Arigato! Arigato!!*"

"Good news?" Maya asked.

"Fuck yeah," Glenn answered. "My buddy Taka is coming to pick us up. You remember Taka? He knows where we are. He says it'll take him 40 minutes to get here."

The jubilation came and went again as we sat and waited, bewildered by just how the hell we got ourselves into this mess. Glenn and I seemed to have a talent for getting stranded out in the cold. He and Nat collapsed into an exhausted heap on one of the benches outside the station while Maya and I huddled together on another to beat the cold, listening to the clock tick until our savior arrived. A half hour passed and I thought for sure she'd fallen asleep. Then she mumbled through her scarf.

"You're pretty good at this, you know."

"At what?"

"Cuddling. Some people do it all wrong."

"Not me, huh?"

She squeezed my arm a bit harder. "No, you feel good."

"Aww, you guys make such a cute couple!" Glenn interrupted. I didn't even know he was awake over there.

She leaned away, the cold air creeping between us again. "We're not a couple."

"You're wearing his hat, aren't you?"

She didn't have time to respond to that genius observation, because just then the darkness was severed by approaching headlights.

Glenn gave Taka an enormous hug when he pulled up, right on time, but the reunion was brief. We didn't want to take up any more of the man's time than absolutely necessary, and he looked like he'd gotten out of bed just to do us this favor. Even so, the smile on his face said he was happy to oblige. He and Glenn chatted up front the entire trip back to Kuma (mostly about music), as if nothing out of the ordinary was going down. Loyalty, courtesy, and a calm demeanor were highly-valued traits here, but damn. Japanese friends are there when you need them.

Sure wish I'd made some.


I walked back to Glenn's place after dropping Maya off at the train station the next morning, spirits high and nothing but Fuji on my mind. We spent most of the day like a couple of true stoners, watching old episodes of *South Park* and leaving only to pick up ramen, smokes, and yellow Gatorade. Glenn spent much of the afternoon on the phone with Natsumi arranging the logistics for the next day.

"Nice!" he blurted out in response to a text. "Riley says he's in."

The plan was to begin the hike at sunset and walk through the night to catch dawn at the summit. Watching the sun come up over the Japanese countryside atop the highest mountain in the land was one of the most spectacular sites on earth, if the legends were to be believed. On top of everything, I got confirmation that Glenn and Nat would not be joining me and Celine on our trip to Southeast Asia, so this would be the last time he and I would hang out before we both went back to the real world. This made me doubly glad we were finally doing this. Best to send our friendship off in style.

"Hey," Natsumi said suddenly from behind the wheel, just under three hours into the drive. She turned off the music and pointed ahead with her dark eyes, which had gone wide. *"Mite.* (Look.)*"*

Glenn leaned forward to peer out the windshield. "Whoa," was all he could manage. The highway veered towards the left and something terrible drifted into view off to the right. My head turned to meet it. Looming like a massive boil on the face of mother earth, *Fuji-san* greeted us with its towering might on full display in the distance, thirsting to crush any fool who dared to trespass.

The base of the mountain could have been a hundred miles wide. It began with a gentle, linear ascent from the flat surrounding terrain before gradually increasing its steepness with near parabolic symmetry on either side. I extended an L-shape with my thumb and forefinger out the window and estimated a nearly 45-degree incline on the approach to the summit. Since it was August and there was no snow at the top, the whole thing resembled a titanic pile of rust-colored dirt, like the bottom half of some great celestial hourglass waiting to be flipped again. And, of course, it was an active volcano. A small bowling ball dropped from my throat to my belly when I tried to picture an actual human being up there somewhere.

"We should probably stretch," Glenn said.

Perhaps unsurprisingly, my thoughts went to JRR Tolkien – this place was straight out of the world of high fantasy. I couldn't decide which of the evil mountains of Middle Earth Fuji most resembled – Caradhras, highest and foulest peak of the Misty Mountains; the Lonely Mountain, nesting place of the calamitous dragon Smaug; or Mount Doom, furnace of Sauron and spewer of hellfire. Whichever the case, Frodo and company were in for some shit.

The mountain is divided into ten stations, with number ten at the bottom and one at the summit. Visitors can drive up as high as the fifth station and find parking. From there the only way up is on foot. We arrived as the last light of day vanished and discovered Riley had already arrived. 'Twas a merry meeting of Hobbits. He'd brought two British friends with him, both of whom were nice enough, but the introductions were brief and I don't recall their names. We already had everything packed, so the six of us strapped on our boots and whipped out our walking sticks. The stars were bright, the air was crisp, and the excitement was palpable. We were about to conquer Mount Fuji!

Thus began the second worst night of my life.


The group managed to stay together for the first ninety minutes or so, but Riley and his lads were in far better shape than the three of us. They let us take point at the beginning, but by the end of the second hour they'd overtaken us and were long gone. As hour three passed and we approached Station 7, the desolation of the landscape began to take its toll psychologically.

A heavy fog rolled in and all sound seemed to cease. Except for the occasional fellow climber passing by, there was no life in any direction. No plants, birds, or small mammals of any kind that normally contributed to an earthly biological ecosystem. This was an *active volcano,* owing its enormity to layer upon layer of lava, ash, and dust that had been belched out for millennia and deposited upon its barren slopes.

"The very air you breathe is a poisonous fume," the grim voice of Boromir uttered in the deep places of my mind. I couldn't help but find a dark humor in our plight. I shared my little "Hobbits in Mordor" fantasy with Glenn and Natsumi.

"Watch out for that Gollum, y'all!" Glenn laughed. "You know he's following us."

Nat joined in. "Wait, who has the precious?"

"I got the precious."

"No you don't, I do."

"*Liar!!*"

The nerdy banter kept our spirits up for almost another hour, but before long we lost the energy to converse and were devoured by an all-consuming silence.


Somewhere during the approach to Station 8 a twinge in my groin shot an explosive burst of pain up the left side of my midsection. I buckled over and sat on the nearest large rock. Glenn and Nat caught up to me a couple minutes later, both hurting in their own way, and planted themselves next to me. Glenn's expression was difficult to read, but his body language left no doubt his main battery was at zero percent and he was running on emergency power. Nat looked downright homicidal, drenched in sweat and shaking from the cold. Out of nowhere, my buddy sprung up and gave his best halftime speech to his down-and-out team, then turned to the next lurcher-by and asked him in busted Japanese to take a photo of the three of us.

He threw his arms around me and Nat and conjured the most cheeseball grin in the history of photography, which was somehow contagious. The photo came out with the three of us grimacing like buffoons, bloodshot eyes and bared teeth chattering. Three strung-out corpses at the end of our ropes. It remains to this day the image of myself in which I am by far the most unhappy. There are baby photos of me bawling in the bathtub. They don't come close.

Around the seventh hour on the mountain it started – not raining, exactly, but more like *misting*. That soft, irritating spray that comes at you sideways, making it impossible to shield your face from it. Like a true noob I hadn't packed anything waterproof, so I had to just suck it up as my 100% cotton Clutch hoodie turned into a wet towel. It didn't matter. It was summit or die.

I pushed myself up, leaning hard on my walking so my arms and shoulders could take some of the weight off my feet. Every step was painful, so I took a break nearly every time a suitable rock presented itself. The others took no issue with this as they matched my sloth-like pace in silent misery. Progress was slow and excruciating.

you're only in hell because you're in terrible shape and totally weak.

*Weak? We're climbing a freakin' mountain!*

At last we reached the penultimate station – the final stretch before victory. Strangely, however, there were a lot more climbers on the trail than before. More and more appeared, as if materializing from the dirt, and before long it was straight-up *crowded.*

"Where the hell did all these people come from?" I shouted to the sky.

"Hotel," Nat answered with a grunt.

"Hotel??"

"*Hai.* If you have money and make a reservation like five years before, you can sleep on the mountain in a little hotel."

We rounded the next bend and there it stood – the "Station Nine Inn" or refuge or sanctuary or whatever the hell it was called. This stripped-down bungalow of sorts had no justifiable existence on the side of this volcano. Its shitbag guests had climbed to station nine during the day and had been sleeping comfortably through the night only to emerge an hour before dawn to make the summit by sunrise.

There were so many of them, in fact, that to get to the top we now had to wait in a *queue.* We'd climbed all night only be stopped in our tracks moments from victory by a wall of rich tourists. Luckily for them, homicide requires that the perpetrator be in command of his physical faculties. I blew a big fat raspberry instead.

that'll show 'em.

There was nothing to be done. We got in line and waited, soaked to the bone and aching all over. The first traces of light appeared through the fog as dawn approached. Every minute or so we took a step forward, each of which sent shocks up my shattered groin muscles.

Out of desperation, I tried to meditate. I once saw a documentary where a wizened old Shaolin monk stood for hours on his fingertips and broke earthenware bowls with his dick. Mind over matter, right?

Wrong. I pulled out all the old tricks. I conjured the orb and slammed the Bruce Lee fist. Nothing. I called to mind Seoan and Ambient Nights and summoned the flickering image of Celine's candle. Nada. Each step forward delivered an agonizing jolt that brought me back to my grim reality. I couldn't just meditate pain away. I'd need a lifetime of training for that.

The fog suddenly turned orange, as though a spectral mist of Fanta had descended, and we knew the sun had just broken the horizon. This should have been my moment, the grand prize at the end of the marathon – standing witness to the infinite glory of sunrise atop Mt. Fuji. And here I was, soaking wet and miserable, standing in line like an asshole. Not exactly how I'd imagined it. I couldn't even see the top of the mountain, so there was no telling how much longer it would take to get to the summit. I just wanted to go back to bed.

To hell with this volcano, to hell with the view, to hell with these tourist bastards, to hell with life on Earth and the human race. May we all drown in a fiery pool of liquid-hot magma.

Another hour went by and we were still in line.

"Fuck this," Glenn muttered for the hundredth time. He'd joined me in mentally checking out of this wretched place. Nat was leaning on him, eyes closed and completely gone. The orange had turned to pale gray by then, that typical color of fog in the morning when nothing particularly eventful is happening. An apt metaphor for our time and place.

At long last, the end of the line crept into view high above. There were only about forty people in front of us and they were moving in more quickly than before. The sunrise had come and gone and people were leaving now.

And so, after eight grueling hours of climbing, the three of us crossed the threshold onto the summit of Mt. Fuji, bruised, battered, and defeated. It shouldn't have taken more than six. A makeshift cafeteria off to the left was buzzing with burnt-out-looking hikers all scrambling to get food in a surprisingly orderly fashion. Without a word, the three of us clomped over to the corner, let our bags fall to the ground and collapsed heads-down on the nearest empty table.


I couldn't guess how long we stayed there, but it was still morning when I pulled my head up again. We slowly lurched back to the land of the living and took in the scene around us. The bright colors of people in hiking gear poked through the fog, some of which were moving about quietly while others had collapsed as we had. The only sound was the clinking and clattering of bowls and chopsticks – they served ramen at this place and there was no shortage of business. Outside the cafeteria there was no telling what lay in which direction, but the crater must have been close.

"Anyone hungry?" Glenn asked, breaking the silence.

Nat looked over at the crowd of people waiting for food. "No more lines."

"Yeah, screw that," Glenn agreed. "You guys want to try to find the crater?"

Two heads shook.

"Alright, let's just go."

Two heads nodded. We were done.

Oh, wait... no, we weren't. There was still the three-hour hike back down.

*But surely hiking down is a breeze compared to going up?*

You'd think so, but active volcanos are essentially humungous piles of gravel. That meant slipping and sliding and stones in every shoe, with some high-velocity face plants if you missed your step. The good news was that a person could plummet down the mountain in leaps and bounds, making incredible time if they were careful about it. The gravel acted as a natural brake against the downwards momentum, so gravity did most of the work. The bad news was that every footfall in this manner was a shock to the musculoskeletal system. Not much fun with a pulled muscle. I had at least nine.

Regardless, leaping down the side of a volcano at breakneck speed is not something a person gets to do every day. Despite the stabbing pain in my leg, the contrast between this and waiting in line to go up was magnificent. After being bullied mercilessly for eight long hours we finally got to stick it to the mountain. Every crunch of gravel underfoot was a little, *"Screw you, Fuji!"* I didn't fall once.

Reaching the tree line again was a return to Eden. Life

appeared where for so long had been only death. I heard birds and running water. I smelled pine needles in the air and felt lovely, lovely dirt under my boots. I tore off my drenched hoodie as the sun came out, injecting its benevolent warmth directly to my core, right down to the gonads. The pace slowed way down as we approached the end of this whole shit show, my only thought being how I might literally murder someone if I didn't get a shower. I'd been sweating bricks the whole way down and every exposed scrap of skin was coated in a suffocating layer of grit.

The moment I'd been waiting for finally arrived and I found myself back where I'd started a lifetime ago. My body at last succumbed to exhaustion. I collapsed onto asphalt while I waited for Glenn and Natsumi. Never was a parking lot so soothing.

I spent those few minutes alone in pure delirium, drowning in a traumatic cocktail of relief, joy, self-pity, rage, and fatigue I pray never to experience again. Footsteps approached from somewhere and Nat's voice broke the silence.

"Well," she groaned. "They say a wise man climbs Mount Fuji, and only a fool climbs it twice."

Some minutes later the three of us were back in the car, pulling away from that God-forsaken mountain, silent, broken, and not at all looking forward to the three-hour drive back to Kumagaya. I have no idea how Nat managed to stay awake enough to operate a vehicle, but she stepped up like a champ.

I took one last look behind from the back seat and gave a quiet nod of respect to the monstrosity that had inflicted such terrible wounds of body and spirit. As I turned away again, in neither triumph nor defeat, the Gremlin got in one last word.

*i can't believe you missed the crater.*

The next day passed in a slow cloud of cannabis smoke and stand-up comedy back in Kumagaya. At some point Riley appeared and took a seat, sizing up how well we'd fared the mountain with a grin that was somehow both condescending and empathetic. The far quicker pace he and his crew had set had gotten them to the top well in time for sunrise, though the thick cloud cover had denied him the prize-winning view just as it had everyone else. Regardless, he still managed to make us feel like we had achieved something extraordinary and should be proud of ourselves, offering hearty congratulations all around for even making it to the top. For the rest of our lives, he said, we could say that we'd climbed Mount Fuji – and that was pretty slick. This wasn't exactly an earth-shattering insight, but it cheered me up to hear him say it.

My body protested every move the next morning as I got ready to head back to Hiroshima. I think this took my attention away from the moment at hand, which I was almost grateful for. Glenn had been my best friend at a critical time in my life, an ever-present escape hatch whenever I felt the pressures bearing down on me, and our paths were unlikely to ever cross again. My most unique friendship by far had reached its expiration date.

We lit up a couple of Camel Lights and walked down to the front of his building. If he ever found himself around my way in lower mid-Atlantic USA, I told him, he should give me a ring and I'd show him the spots. He extended the same invite to his neck of the woods in the Southwest before giving me a bear hug that made my spine crack. The force of it caused me to drop my cigarette into a puddle that had formed the night before. He gave me a new one. A horrible silence passed as I searched for something to say that would close out our relationship in some meaningful way, but I had nothing. I shook his hand for the last time and we parted ways with a simple, "Good times."

Damn right they were.

My legs had cramped up again by the time I reached the station, so I took a moment at the top of stairs to offer a silent thank-you to Kumagaya, my magical little sanctuary city that always greeted me with a beer and a smooch. The name would remind me of my old friend until the end of time, as though Glenn had it tattooed on his arm.

I lurched onto the train, melting into the first empty seat I saw. Gravity had never pulled so hard. As we drifted forward and the view changed from city to country, the Gremlin grumbled. The awful thing that had just happened with Glenn was also going to happen with Maya and Celine, and by summer's end there would be two more festering vacuums in my soul. My eyes floated as the scene played out in my head again and again.

This was the price of the expat life – it's heavy on farewells and they all cut deeper than you think they will. Somewhere between Tokyo and Osaka I made a promise to keep in contact with them once real life began and we all had boring desk jobs back in the West. All I could do was try my best to keep it.

# FISH IN THE SEA

Chris Rock had a bit about soul mates in his *Never Scared* HBO special, which came out that same year. In a nutshell, he said, they don't exist. Sorry, folks, forget the soul. All you can hope for is a mate. Nobody ever finds a perfect match and lives happily ever after. Real life always wins out. Even if you do meet the right person, it won't be the right time.

Those last five weeks in Hiroshima zipped by with the familiar quickness of any given summer. Maya and I spent most of our free time outdoors enjoying the late sun and warm nights, especially down by the riverfront. The arcade was buzzing with food vendors and she made me finally try *tako yaki*, which I'd been avoiding for damn near two years. Deep-fried octopus balls just weren't something I wanted in my mouth. You can imagine my surprise when it turned out to be delicious. How could I have denied myself this wonderful earthly pleasure for so long?

"Told you so," Maya smiled.

I nodded. "It's good, I'll admit it. But it can't touch *okonomi yaki.*"

"Maybe," Maya said, then held up the kebob stick. "Easier to eat, though!"

*Okonomi yaki* had long since become my favorite Japanese street food. The thing is essentially an omelet, made up of cabbage, assorted meats, egg, and some sort of batter that allows it to be prepared and eaten like a giant pancake. You sit at a counter with a grill built into the countertop and place your order with the chef on the other side. He then pours the batter on the grill in front of you (hibachi-style) and tosses handfuls of random stuff (mainly cabbage) into it, lays down the meat and squirts on the sauces. It then gets fried up, flipped over and presented to you, whereupon you add your choice of even more toppings and dig into it with a putty knife. The burst of flavors is wondrous to behold – a mystical medley that is both savory and sweet, satisfying cravings for carbs, meats, seafood, veggies, fast food, or all of the above.

Living in Japan was a constant internal battle over deciding what to eat. With so many good options it was hard to even know what I was in the mood for. Sushi nearly always won out, but during the summer when the vendors were out in force it was tough to resist the call of the grill. The decision nearly always fell on me since Maya was the indecisive type. Since I was more impulsive, on several occasions we ended up with a mouthful of something uniquely revolting.

One night downtown we were talking about movies and I let it slip that I'd never seen *E.T.* As a huge film buff, I had no acceptable rationale for missing such an iconic motion picture. At first Maya didn't believe me, but by then she knew me well enough to catch when I was bullshitting. Most of the time. Her incredulity gave way to righteous indignation – like she took it as a personal slight that I'd never seen it – and she demanded an immediate viewing. She led us straightaway to the nearest video store (these were easy to spot) and back to her apartment to watch. By then it was already past midnight and it would be a struggle to stay awake for a whole movie, but I didn't care. There wasn't much about that particular children's classic I found terribly captivating in the first place, so no harm done if I slept through it.

After Maya struggled with the RCA connector for a few minutes she threw herself down next to me on the futon, gave me a weird little smile and threw her arms around my belly. This was a clear sign that things between her and the boyfriend back home weren't going well – she only got this affectionate after an email argument or whatever else was making her second-guess the whole relationship. I wondered if I should ask her about it.

"I just wanna cuddle," she said, as if anticipating my question.

The music crescendos pretty loud at the end of *E.T.* when the spaceship blasts away. I'm pretty sure that's what woke me up, with no recollection of the movie and staring half-asleep at the credits rolling by. I glanced down at Maya, who had at some point thrown a pillow in my lap and fallen asleep on it, and saw my fingers buried in her hair. As I carefully pulled them out and beheld the tangled mess, out of nowhere came a burst of laughter I couldn't stifle. I threw a hand over my mouth, mortified. She stirred and looked up at me with a barely perceptible "*Hmm?*" sound, then smiled and fell back asleep. I sat there for a while just watching her breathe, undeniably gorgeous from head to toe. Right as I was about to drift back to sleep myself, the Gremlin muttered something awful.

you really blew it with this one, Romeo.

No matter how close we'd grown since February, a romantic relationship with Maya had never seemed possible. With the end of my time in Japan fast approaching, I'd always managed to talk myself out of the idea. But it wasn't just the lousy timing. Maybe I had some moral reservations about her being in a serious (albeit long-distance) relationship, or some unconscious belief that she was out of my league. Or maybe I understood that a true friend, especially one in a foreign land, was too valuable to risk losing with that sort of thing.

no, you just never had the balls to make a move.

*Oh, fuck off.*

For the next twenty-four hours it was like the Gremlin had stumbled onto the Red Cross's emergency supply of crystal meth. It snarled with a ferocity I hadn't heard since the little bastard tried to talk me into leaving Japan back in Nagaoka. Its words were as insidious as they were then, threatening me now with the foulest thing a human being can experience – *regret*. If I didn't become Maya's personal love monkey I'd never forgive myself, not ever. It screamed at me a million and a half reasons why I should put it all on the line, acting entirely out of character and tossing whatever self-respect I had right to the wind.

No. I wasn't about to attempt some lust-fueled, hail Mary scheme to connive my way uninvited into Sexytown. Even if by some miracle she actually went for it, there were no scenarios at the end of that road that would make it worth it. I was clueless about her boyfriend back in Canada; for all I knew he was the real deal. Was I going to screw up their future together for the sake of some ill-fated, three-week long tryst? Guilt like that was a cancer. I didn't need that shit in my life.

but she's just so... so...

*Yes, she is. But it wasn't meant to be. Now let's get our head out of the gutter and try to enjoy the little time that's left.*

There's nothing easy about trying to ignore an infatuation. The whole function of the brain changes, setting the object of your desire as your new default mental background like an endless, looping screensaver. The worst part is that even if you try your utmost, like literally bang your head against the wall to get them out of your mind, only half of you really wants to. The other half, down where the Gremlin lurks, lives in a dizzying haze of irrational sentimentality, falling over itself trying to entertain the fantasy for as long as humanly possible. How's *that* for yin and yang?

I was lucky enough by then to have built up a pretty decent defense mechanism against this sort of cognitive dissonance. That was meditation's greatest gift to me. Plus, I had my big adventure in Southeast Asia if I needed a change of focus. I was very, very grateful to have these things in my arsenal. The idea of being with Maya wasn't easily driven from the mind.

But I had to try. I didn't stop talking to her or anything drastic like that – I loved spending time with her and time was short. So, we kept on enjoying the street food and the summer nights, the riverfront and the occasional Mai Tai, as good friends do. All else was kept caged away with the Gremlin in its dark hole where it damn well belonged.


My manager arranged a going-away party for me the day before I left. She treated the entire staff from all three LUNA schools in Hiroshima to three hours in a private room at her favorite karaoke facility. Even Vivian made it out to this one, and intended to take full advantage of a rare night away from the kids. She and Maya were three drinks in and already howling along to Bon Jovi when I arrived. Being a civilized being, I limited my own repertoire to more dignified selections of the Blink-182 variety.

Afterwards, those of us who were happiest the weekend had landed decided to keep the party going. This was my last hurrah, after all, and I was in no rush for it to end. There were five of us – myself, Vivian and Maya, and two other JTs, Mika and Satomi. Mika-sensei led us a few blocks upriver to a club called *El Barco,* one of her go-to spots for dancing the night away. The place wasn't much more than a basement, reeking of sweat, tobacco, and whatever other foulness had accumulated in the ducts over the years. The haze of smoke was blinding, all sound was lost to meteoric bass lines, and I had to scream my throat sore just to order a shot at the bar. It was, in all ways, a fine venue.

The music was very much on point, showcasing the great artists of the era – Dirty Vegas, DJ Sammy, Princess Superstar, you name it. The dance floor lit up as the five of us took it over, drawing increasing stares from the locals as the night wore on and inhibitions faded.

I was smoking a butt in a booth by the wall when Afroman dropped. Cheers went up with the first measure of "Because I Got High," and eventually my eyes landed on Maya and Vivian. They were dancing slow, arms locked and screaming along with the lyrics, despite knowing only the infamous refrain. Mika and Satomi had vanished. Through the blackness Maya caught my eye in a strobe flash and made a high-speed beeline towards me, pulled me up by the lapel and dragged me over to join them. I was saved by good timing as the beat faded out moments after we rejoined Vivian. I hated that song.

Just then Vivian decided to call it a night. We'd been raging pretty hard and she just wasn't used to that anymore, she said, and would probably need a week to sleep it off. It didn't take a genius to see she might have a tough time making her way home. So, after she paid her tab Maya and I walked her back outside and flagged down a taxi for her. She threw open the door with inordinate force, then spun around to bid me "nice-to-meet-you-and-goodbye" with a big group hug. We emerged again and Vivian stood there beaming at us.

"You two should totally hook up," she blurted out.

I gaped like a shubunkin – awkwardness of that magnitude is a potent cocktail when you're not ready for it. Vivian must have picked up on that vibe, because her smile dropped as soon as she'd said it. She turned without another word, flopped into the cab, and was gone. After one or two stupefied seconds I turned away from the street again, avoiding eye contact with Maya like an insecure jackass. I could still feel the thoracic pulse of subterranean bass from the club behind us. Part of me wanted to race back in and vanish into the music.

"I'm gonna go," she sighed. There was no hint of embarrassment in her voice, only exhaustion. The energy had left her and her guard had dropped.

"I'll take you home," I said.

"Ooh, such a gentleman!" she teased, pinching my shoulder hard. "You're just trying to get some booty, aren't you?"

I busted out laughing, not so much at the irony of the question but that sweet, good-natured Maya had actually invoked the term "booty." The weirdness faded as we hopped into the next cab. Like many foreign teachers (myself included), Maya kept her home address written in Japanese on a piece of paper always close at hand. She showed this to the driver. He gave a quick thumbs-up and we were off.

The route to Maya's neighborhood cut right through downtown. The Peace Park and A-Bomb Dome quietly approached, bathed in its nightly emerald glow, as if waiting to bid me farewell. I watched out the rear window as it sank away into the distance, taking a piece of my soul along with it. If that was the price of forgiveness, I'd pay it gladly.

I heaved a heavy sigh. Maya leaned in and put her head on my shoulder as if she'd read every word behind it.

"I can't believe you're leaving me," she murmured. "You're my best friend here." Words failed me as she took my hand. I had no idea how I was going to say goodbye to this glorious soul I'd barely just met. In another life I would have followed her anywhere.

"What's the first thing you're gonna do when you get home?" she asked.

"Find myself a decent martini and shoot some pool," I replied with forced cheerfulness. She snickered at this in a slightly condescending, "boys will be boys" kind of way.

"What about you?" I asked as the taxi pulled up to her building. My heart jumped as she opened the door before we'd stopped. The driver hit the brakes and threw a cutting look over his shoulder.

"*Gomennesai!* (Sorry!)" I shouted. I paid him quickly and walked around to where Maya was still sitting in the back seat with the door open, ruing the day she was ever introduced to Mr. Steven P. Vodkatonic. She kept it together long enough for me to help her onto her feet. As the taxi pulled away, I cursed her horrible, stairs-only building. She lived on the sixth floor.

We crossed the parking lot to the stairs and Maya yanked her hand away from mine, taking the first flight at a run. Apparently she was feeling better. At the bottom of the second flight she stopped and hung her head, holding on to the railing for support. Apparently not. She reluctantly acquiesced to me helping her up the rest of the way. After a slow, steady march up to the top we arrived at her door and I reflected upon what an uncelebrated gift to humanity is the elevator.

Her apartment was spotless. Maya never struck me as the OCD type, but she'd definitely attacked the place with Pine Sol that day. I made brief mention of this and she threw up her hands in a kind of *"Voilá!"* motion. She then spun on a dime and high-tailed it to the bathroom. The sounds of regurgitation soon echoed off the walls. Buzzing pretty hard myself I fell onto the futon, thinking I should at least wait to make sure she didn't pass out over the toilet before I left. Several flushes later the stirrings of life could be heard again, including the running of the tap, the opening and closing of cabinets, and the brushing of teeth.

*"Okay, time's up,"* I thought to myself, dreading the moment. *"Just say goodbye and go. Don't drag it out."*

Just then Maya emerged from the bathroom, looking good as new. She crossed the room, fell to her knees beside me, and pressed her lips against mine.

Rhyme and reason went out the window as I savored the intoxicating medley of cherry lip gloss, vodka, and Listerine. God knows how long we stayed like that, not that it mattered. I just wanted time to stop. We eventually pulled apart and just looked at each other for a while. Something inside me was collapsing.

"Why now?" the Gremlin asked, stealing my voice.

Not taking her eyes off mine, she took a deep breath and slowly let it out again, managing one last smile as her hand went to my cheek.

"I dunno," she whispered, pulling me towards her. She

kissed me again, soft and slow, then quietly flopped over onto the futon and passed out.

Life isn't exactly HBO, and not every season ends with the closure we hope for. I don't recall leaving her place that night or how I got back to my part of town, but I somehow wound up at the river fighting the urge to jump in and drown. Maya's goodbye had ripped me open, shattering my defenses as the reality of everything ending washed over me in a crushing torrent. It just didn't seem real – how could my time in Japan be over? My thoughts flew to Celine and Glenn, Chantelle and Silvia, all my students, trainers, and fellow teacher-soldiers. An agonizing love for every one of them streamed out the corners of my eyes.

I gazed out in triumph from my balcony in Nagaoka, listened to Moby ignite the new year in Tokyo, and gave endless high-fives to little Hinako-chan. My heart sang to orange clouds on Mt. Fuji, human tides at Shibuya, and one-way trains to the wrong damn place. Nothing that was before me could ever compare to what I was leaving behind – a thousand and one extraordinary people, places, and experiences fate had blessed me with, undeservedly and unconditionally, in this brief time that would exist only in the pages of an old journal and my own fading memory.

# THAILAND

"Hey, loser!" Celine greeted me at the airport, already decked out in tropical vacation garb.

"Sup, beeyotch!" I spat back, and we were all caught up. Celine didn't do hugs.

We had ten days. Our flight would take us from Tokyo to Krabi, Thailand, with a brief stopover in Bangkok. Neither of us had ever been to the Thai capital, but we chose to forego the big city and make straight for the islands in the south of the country. Now, before you begin your reprimand, let me assure you that skipping Bangkok was no easy decision. Celine and I were well aware of the city's reputation as a domain of urban weirdness not to be missed by anyone with an even mildly adventurous spirit. We pondered long the wisdom of spending one of our precious few vacation days there at the expense of an extra one down south, but ultimately decided in the negative. We were lusting for the quiet serenity of sand, sun, and booze-filled coconuts. Bangkok could wait until our paths crossed again.

And yes, to the gentleman in the back wearing the "Chiang Mai Forever" T-shirt, we made the same decision about that city as well. Please sit down.

Krabi. Most people are only familiar with its counterpart on the other side of the bay, Phuket, made famous by its glorious spelling and that episode of Lost where Jack gets the evil tattoo. Krabi is Phuket's less-touristy Siamese twin, home to white sand beaches, clear coastal seas, and (like anywhere in Thailand) mouth-watering foodstuffs.

Then there was Ko Phi Phi, the delightfully-named islands 40 kilometers off the southern coast. These two little specks on the map had become global phenomena after a bite from a parasitic organism called Hollywood. The 1998 movie *The Beach* starring a pre-*Titanic* Leo DiCaprio was shot at a place called Maya Bay on the smaller of the two islands, Phi Phi Le, providing a truly spectacular backdrop. The film had turned the island into a tourist gravity well so powerful that even weirdos like Celine and I were helpless against its pull, and Krabi was one of the jumping-off points to get there from the mainland. There we'd have four glorious days of relaxing by the water and who-the-hell-cares what else. Figuring in one full day of travel each way, that left three days at the end to change gears and wrap things up.

We landed in Bangkok on September 5, 2004. A burst of hot, aggressively humid air blitzed me from the gap between the cabin door and the jet bridge, and my body knew it was on vacation.

Tourists were everywhere, most of whom were a mixed bag of young people in their 20s and 30s from all over the world. The air was thick with languages I didn't recognize, but my ears automatically zoned in on anyone speaking English and began eavesdropping. I overheard conversations I had zero interest in, but for some reason they cut through the background chatter to hold my attention with surprising force. Celine was getting that, too.

"Yah, isn't it weird?" she said. "It's like all the Americans are just louder and more obnoxious than everyone else. Imagine that!"

"Don't you have a moose to hunt or something?"

"Ha!"

It didn't take long for us to start making fun of people's conversations. What better way to kill three hours before our connecting flight to Krabi? Lousy tourists... clearly they were all morons. Not at all like us.

As we sat lazily in the wake of Pad Thai and Singha beer, an odd-looking man suddenly sat down next to us and struck up a conversation in a thick British accent. He'd just wrapped up a lengthy stint at the beaches, the stubble on his head bleached by exposure and skin tanned to a leathery crisp. His huge pupils suggested he was still off his teat from whatever pharmaceutical concoction he'd been enjoying. He'd attended not one, but *three* of Thailand's notorious Full Moon parties and claimed to have found true love at the last one. His dream girl had already left for London and he was hot on her tail after they'd pledged themselves to each other a few days ago. He described her inconceivable beauty in

Shakespearean terms, confessing he never thought he'd find his soul mate in this life. And he swore it wasn't just the drugs talking.

Celine was enraptured by the story and had turned to silly putty. "That's so sweeeeet!" she kept interrupting.

"This bloke is in for a hard reality check when he arrives clear-eyed and sober back in London," I thought. He seemed nice enough, though, so I kept that to myself. Besides, I wanted to hear more about the party.

"So, tell us about the Full Moon," I said. "Does it live up to its reputation?"

He closed his eyes as if recalling a one-night stand with Helen of Troy, then took a deep breath and launched into a long-winded tale of earthly pleasures and heavenly music. Evidently, A-list DJs from around the world flocked to the Full Moon parties every year and strove to outdo each other. He spoke of blistering three-hour sets of drum & bass, spirit-throttling trip-hop and downtempo, and wanton acts of carnality on the dance floor during early-morning stretches of deepest house. I was ready to buy my ticket right then and there.

Then he showed us the photos.

Far from the tropical euphoria he made it out to be, the photos revealed the worst kind of cash-grabber tourist trap. The people in them were nearly all foreigners who had laid waste to the beach, cramped together like sardines stomping on a thick carpet of beer cans and garbage. I'd been to plenty of shitty, hyper-commercialized music festivals that I'd shelled out megabucks to attend, only to find stages built on landfills, human walls at every turn, porta potties tipping over, and half-mile lines to buy $14 pretzels with no salt. I winced at the undeniable evidence that these "legendary" parties had been infected in equal measure by the same slithering parasites of corporate avarice. Hard pass.

"Looks like fun, man," I said, handing the camera to Celine. Her face was stoic as she scrolled through the pictures. I could practically smell the revulsion beneath the façade.

We wished him the best of luck with his true love as he abruptly sprung up from his chair and left to find new ears to fill.

"Buncha burnouts," Celine uttered. "That did *not* look like fun."

I imagined it was tons of fun before it went bad, overrun by ever-increasing invasions of loud, inconsiderate foreign riffraff who looked just like the two of us. I vowed then and there to never perpetuate that stereotype. Maybe I was being a pompous asshole, but I was okay with that.


It was the smallest, shakiest plane I'd ever taken, but it got us to Krabi in one piece. We jumped into a cab and were hotel-bound, stupefied by the awesome beauty of the landscape that passed by with the open-window breeze. Monstrous cliffs burst from the earth all around us and leapt to the stratosphere. The bare rock was spotted with patches of dark green upwards along their sides before being crowned by plateaus of dense canopy jungle hundreds of feet above. What tumultuous geological processes could have created this kind of sheerness in the otherwise flat topography? It was by far the most exotic landscape I'd ever seen.

The sun was getting low in the sky when we pulled up to the hotel and Celine gave a squeal of delight – a baby elephant was puttering around by the entrance to the lobby. There he stood, unaccompanied and unmarked, enjoying the afternoon and not making a fuss. The li'l fella barely noticed as I cautiously approached, patted his midsection, and gave a quick thumbs up to Celine, who had whipped out her camera. He suffered the photo with dignity, but was otherwise content to be left alone, thank you very much. I didn't want to take up any more of his time. Besides, Celine and I had a mind to murder some Thai food, so we checked in, dumped our bags in the room, and headed for the restaurant while Mr. Rando McPachyderm turned his attention to other matters. Though our paths did not cross again in this life, I imagine he went on to do great deeds.

We didn't see a single other guest. When I mentioned this to our waitress, she smiled contentedly. It was the middle of the rainy season here and the end of summer in most of the world, she explained, so tourist season was over. Just about everyone had cleared out in the past week or so. This made us even more thrilled to be here, if that were possible.

All of a sudden Celine pointed over my shoulder. "Aww, look at the lizard!"

I turned. Our little green friend was stuck to the side of a cross beam by the ceiling, motionless and minding his own business. A yard or two away there was another, and another. In fact, there were geckos all over the place, hanging out in gravity-defying positions waiting for a tasty bug to mosey along or whatever it is that geckos do up there on the wall.

"Allo, gecko!" I blurted out in an Australian accent.

"Allo, gecko!" Celine echoed with a giggle. Just a couple of Aussies talking to our new gecko friends. The closet one licked its eyeball in greeting.

These geckos were so common to this part of the world that they're actually called the "common house gecko." Often found loitering in closets and bathrooms, they're considered lucky since they eat nasty things like cockroaches and spiders. Our waitress said we'd see zillions of them while we were in Thailand. For some reason this made me happy.

We ordered a round of Mai Tais and something called Tom Ka soup. Neither of us had ever heard of it and we were in the mood to try something new. Our eyes rolled back in our heads as we slurped down the sweet and savory masterpiece, no words exchanged to break our concentration. It had a coconut broth, but I didn't recognize half the other ingredients. It was like someone had walked out to a patch of rainforest in the middle of nowhere, plucked a dozen colorful things from the foliage, and tossed them into a bowl. A perfect blend of delicious and bizarre. The spiciness brought my mouth to the brink of agony before giving way to an herbal-tasting freshness that could have been cilantro, but I'm pretty sure wasn't. Before long I gave up trying to identify all the crispy reds and greens and just surrendered to the experience. Eating soup had never before been such an act of discovery. You just don't often get that in a soup.

"Let's find the pool," Celine murmured as soon as she'd finished.

I gasped. "Have you got a death wish, woman? It hasn't been 30 minutes!"

"So?"

"You are truly mad. I accept."

"You're so friggin' weird."

We came across a gym, another restaurant, a massage parlor, and the front desk three more times before we found what we were looking for. Our hearts sank when we saw the sign on the door.

*Pool hours 8:00 a.m. - 7:00 p.m.*

It was already pushing 9:00 p.m. and the outdoor lights were off, though there was plenty of visibility from a full moon and clear sky. The door wasn't locked and there wasn't a soul about the place.

Not one for tolerating authority in any of its guises, Celine gave a dismissive little snort and charged through the door. I followed, happy that she was still able to read my mind. We took a few steps forward, then stopped as our breath was stolen by the scenery that unfolded before us.

Celine gasped. "Holy fuck."

An enormous flagstone patio stretched out in every direction, opening out to a private section of beach at the far end. Off to the left was an outdoor bar stocking hundreds of bottles, no doubt catering to immense crowds during the dry season. Chaise lounges sparsely populated the borders of a vast, lagoon-style infinity pool that glowed an immaculate turquoise, gently illuminated by submerged lighting that was left on throughout the night. On its right side was a sunken bar ingeniously designed to serve both the pool and the jacuzzi behind it.

In a word... *lush.*

*Seek, and you shall find.*

We slipped into the pool without a sound. The water was predictably delightful, its perfect temperature ensuring that the adrenaline rush that hit me on the way down faded to pure serenity the moment I surfaced again. Celine traversed the entire length of the pool and back again before saying anything.

"Sooooo nice!"

The two of us broke off into our own worlds, lost in thought and contemplating our marvelous luck. Celine had often told me that there was no force in heaven or on earth that gave her more joy than swimming. She hadn't been hyperbolic with that statement – on her face was a look of sheer ecstasy.

I swam to the far end and hung off the edge that looked out onto the beach. Here I gazed upon a body of water known as the Andaman Sea, which meant that this was my first-ever glimpse of the Indian Ocean. The moonlight sparkled off her like a disco ball and I smiled back in greeting.

My eyes began to adjust and silhouettes took shape all around, the brightness of the moon casting nighttime shadows on the sand. The beach itself was framed with geometric precision by twin lines of palm trees that approached from either side and swayed gently in the breeze. Overhead, a celestial explosion littered the heavens with a trillion shining dots. The low-hanging moon was so perfectly positioned that its beam traced a clear path of illumination straight from the horizon, across the sea, up the beach, and right into the pool. I cleared my head to meditate and the full power of the vista crashed in like a tidal wave.

How could I possibly be here? Was this all just a gift? A lesson of some sort? Was I being pranked by the universe, given this sweetest taste of life tonight only to be run over by a cement mixer in the morning? Was there any meaning to it, or had chaos alone brought me here?

A gentle splashing sound emerged as Celine swam around behind me. Something about hearing her, or perhaps just knowing she was there, added even greater serenity to the moment. She wasn't part of the vision of nature before my eyes, but her presence elsewhere in my perception was comforting. I was left with a sense of both cosmic solitude and priceless friendship, as if I were able to share something extraordinary with someone who was only partly there. It was the best of both worlds – oneness with all creation and a deep connection to another living soul. I drank it all down in gigantic gulps, offering a silent thanks to anyone listening. Time went up in smoke.

Celine's voice floated through the silence. "You look soooo happy!"

My eyes didn't move from the beach. "Yes… this is… a good spot. Come look." I motioned for her to join me, still gazing in meditation at the watery horizon. She swam up and hung her arms over the side of the infinity pool. I could practically *hear* her eyes widen.

"Wow," she whispered.

"Yep."

"Are you just in a total zone right now?"

"Kinda."

"So cool."

The wind picked up and a chorus of trees rustled in the darkness.

"This is where I want to be," I said.

"Totally."

"No, I mean right here. This." I pointed to the beach. "This is where I want to go when I close my eyes. Right here… the beach, the water, the moon, the pool, everything. I want my mind to live here."

Celine didn't reply, but let out another happy sigh and went back to her dog paddling. I stayed there for another few minutes and took a hi-res mental photo of everything around me, making sure that every detail was accounted for and imprinted on my brain. I vowed to revisit it over and over again so that it became etched in my long-term memory. This would be my new fortress of solitude whenever I meditated. If my eyes ever fell shut, I wanted to be transported back to this time and place as if I had a TARDIS parked inside my cerebellum.

I dragged myself away from the scene and came back to reality. This pool was amazing! I gave Celine a little splash before plunging into the depths to do a bunch of underwater somersaults.

I ate my first rambutan at breakfast and was instantly in love. Not just because they're delicious, which they are, but because they're adorable. Rambutans look like little red sea urchins. You wouldn't think there was anything edible about them at first glance – there is a distinctively poisonous look about them, in fact. On the tongue they're a bit like lychees, but tastier and far more charming. The kind of fruit you'd like to take home and introduce to your family. Take a sharp knife around the circumference and inside you'll find a round, fleshy interior that looks like an extra-large, perfectly skinned grape that pops right out of its husk. You can nibble around the pit in the center, or just pop the whole thing into your mouth and suck on it for like 20 minutes. It's juicy and sweet, but not overly so, and there's no sticky mess. Stuff a few of them into your pocket, grab your balisong and you've got yourself a fruity snack for the afternoon.

The ferry ride to Ko Phi Phi was a gorgeous 90-minute glide over the Andaman. A burst of color appeared from the shore as we approached. Buildings painted in vibrant blues, greens, and yellows dotted the landscape, many sporting large signs announcing the names of their establishments. We disembarked onto a fully-functional, western-style beach community that owed its existence to a steady stream of international visitors coming from far and wide.

We took a quick stroll around the village and poked our heads into a few shops. Most were your typical beach bum stores peddling their wares fresh from the sweatshops, though I had to admit some of it was pretty rad. Like a noob I'd forgotten to pack a towel, so I caved and bought an extra-large sarong featuring a huge gecko all in earth tones, much like our little friends back in Krabi. I bought two of them, actually, and a little wooden turtle. And a jade pinky ring.

**tourist.**

*Shut up.*

The village was dotted by dive centers featuring SCUBA and snorkeling excursions out to the various tiny islands in the vicinity. Fortunately, we'd done our homework and knew it was way cheaper to just find someone with a boat to take you around without going through an agency as a middleman. The locals all knew each other and everyone had a friend or relative with a boat. Plus, it was always better to be paid up front in cash without the corporate beak-wetting.

As we walked along the beach back to the pier, we passed youth hostel after youth hostel packed to the brim with characters from what must have been about a hundred nations. Most of them were young, tanned, and good-looking, and either very loudly drunk on the sand or passed out in hammocks hanging from the trees behind. The locals were out and about as well, keeping an eye on their boats, tending shops, or just hanging out in the shade. One of these fellows caught sight of us and spoke a single word.

"Weed?"

"Yep!" Celine responded without hesitation.

you're going to jail.

*Not in this life. Standby law enforcement evasion protocols.*

All the most disturbing scenes from *Midnight Express* played out in my mind as Celine carried out the transaction. I marveled at the ease with which she flouted the law without a thought, and on foreign soil! Being Canadian, she'd no doubt escaped the government-sponsored terror tactics designed to instill rampant anti-drug paranoia in generations of American children. We walked away safe and sound, of course, and a gram or two heavier in the pocket. I was only peeved at her long enough for my heart to stop racing – a few minutes later we were on a longboat taxi circling the island, the wind in our faces and dolphins off the port bow.

We made a final turn around a large rock formation before beginning our approach into Loh Ba Kao Bay, where our hotel was located. We'd coughed up the extra cash to stay at a higher-end place on the far side of the island away from the party animals. The beach was a flawless, 400-yard stretch of white sand, sparkling clean and bordered by a single-file line of palm trees. On either side of the bay stood tall, pointed hills wearing thick coats of dark green foliage from base to summit. Directly ahead we spotted the first line of bungalows about a hundred feet from the water's edge – the most prime real estate in the resort, no doubt.

The sea beneath us turned from navy blue to aquamarine as we crossed the drop-off line. The skipper killed the engine to coast the last hundred feet or so, and we hopped out into the surf like Columbus arriving in the New World. I dug my toes into the sand and listened as tiny waves stumbled onto the shore. A curious notion came to me.

Rich people worked their whole lives for this.

A gigantic wooden map of the resort showed the exact location of our bungalow, about halfway between the gift shop and the pool. We walked along several paths that wound through the place, happily making two or three wrong turns along the way. All of a sudden a chubby green lizard, big enough to swallow a house gecko whole, ran out from behind a bush and stopped in the road in front of us. I prepared myself to answer his riddle or be devoured alive. He scampered off into the underbrush instead.

"I will take that as an omen of splendid times to come," I declared as we arrived at our bungalow.

"Damn right," Celine agreed.

The place looked adorable, like a gigantic brown Lego head wearing a thatched witch's hat. Our bags were waiting for us at the front door. Geckos kept a silent vigil in various spots around the roof.

"Allo, gecko!"

An industrial-strength A/C unit greeted us with a squall of cool air as we stepped inside. It maintained a delightful 68°F, offering a welcome respite from the heat of the afternoon. The room was constructed completely out of wood and decorated all in earth tones, giving it a mellow, rustic feel. The bathroom was lined with a light gray flagstone, with a pair of matching vessel sinks adding a subtle touch of modernity. The oversized bed was bound by blindingly white sheets and covered with pink and red flower petals for a romantic twist. The place was spotless from top to bottom.

Wait... just one bed?

awk-waaaaaard...

*Dude, it's Celine.*

"Sharing a bed, eh?" I said. "Don't you try to take advantage of me, now. You know I'm impressionable and really slutty when I'm drunk."

"Oh, please," Celine hit back. "If I wanted to make you my whore, I would have done it like a year ago."


Sure enough, the concierge had a cousin with a boat. For $150 American he'd take us on a day-long excursion,

221

making a gigantic circle around the island and stopping at all the best snorkeling spots. We'd close out the afternoon with a trip to the famous DiCaprio beach on Maya Bay. It was too good a deal to pass on – we dropped what we were doing and signed on the dotted line. Thirty minutes after breakfast we were shaking his hand and climbing aboard.

It was a great day to be on the water. We cruised around to a half-dozen lagoons, secluded beaches, and rock formations, stopping here and there just to jump over the side and go swimming for a while. I couldn't see a thing with the snorkel, but who cares? We felt like billionaires, galivanting around in our diamond-encrusted yacht whilst every whim was tended to by an adoring public. Our favorite pastime was watching our huge sums of money generate even huger sums of money on Wall Street while we sat back and did nothing to deserve it. We were the lords of all creation, as someone once put it. It was a good fantasy. The truth, of course, was that the skipper was just a cool guy who liked what he did for a living and was happy to be making some unexpected coin that day. The three of us spent much of the time joking about how much better life is at sea than it is on land as we made our approach into Maya Bay.

maya. if only she were here.

*Stop that.*

It was underwhelming. Don't get me wrong, it was a perfectly lovely beach, it just didn't live up to the movie. All the visual effects and groovy soundtrack had given it a kind of ethereal quality on the big screen that just didn't really shine through in the real world. Plus, there was something unsettling about looking out from a beach to see only a tiny speck of open water – nearly all of the view from inside the secluded bay was sheer rock face. It was different and beautiful in its own way, but an endless horizon was part of the heart and soul of a beach. For me, anyway. I loved the feeling of standing at the edge of the world, if only to imagine what it was like long ago when people believed it really was. I just didn't get that feeling there.

"Hollywood totally lied to us," I said to Celine.

"Seriously," she replied. "I think I liked the last one better. Kind of claustrophobic here."

"Right?"

"Oh, well, who gives a shit?" She spun around in the sand. "Everything's still amazing! Fuck Leo DiCaprio!"

"Hey now, watch yourself. That's my boy you're talking about."

"Ha ha, man-crush!"

I tossed her one of those old disposable cameras I'd been lugging around for the occasion. "Here, take a picture."

It came out terribly.

The next morning we were back on a boat to another boat to a taxi to the airport. I'd stocked up on mango soap, coconut shampoo, and some pretty slick-looking jewelry from the gift shop – strictly as gifts for other people, of course – so my bags reeked of exotic tropical fruitiness. We spent the majority of the longboat ride in silence, drinking in the scenery as deeply as we could before saying goodbye to Thailand.

We were loath to put such a place behind us. But we both knew what came next.

# CAMBODIA

Siem Reap is a roughly 500-year-old town on the outskirts of Angkor and the only pocket of modern civilization in the vicinity of the legendary temples. When you visit Angkor, you sleep in Siem Reap.

"Make Angkor your last stop before you leave Asia," Brian had told me months ago during follow-up training. "Make it the grand finale."

We marveled at the number of hotels between the airport and the center of town. The range of options was one of the main factors keeping the rates down, and new ones were in mid-construction all along the main drag. Even indigent scum like Celine and I could afford to stay at a higher-end place without bankrupting ourselves.

Our taxi driver was a jolly old fellow who spoke impressive, albeit broken English. He had two cousins who'd been taking visitors around Angkor for years on their motorcycles and offered us their services for only 25 bucks a day. I hadn't ridden on a motorcycle since I was like ten, so I was super keen on the idea. Celine's brother had given her rides on his bike for years, so motorcycles were familiar territory for her.

They were still working out some of the kinks at our hotel, particularly with the internet. But the rooms were spotless, the water pressure was respectable, and the A/C was absolutely diesel. That last one was key – it was *hot* that day. We didn't even mention the internet fail the next morning, but an extremely apologetic receptionist at the front desk gave us breakfast on the house. A fair trade.

We were greeted with pleasant smiles and good mornings all around as our two pilots arrived and introduced themselves as Han and Solo. They had real names, of course, but their call-signs were such a hit among tourists that the names had stuck. This tickled me to death and I knew it was going to be a great day. Then I noticed there were no helmets.

certain death! our brains will splatter all over the —

*Just get on the bike.*

I climbed on behind Han and we were off. The back of the seat had handrails on either side so it was pretty secure, all things considered. The breeze of the open road caressed my sweaty face as we watched the town pass by in the midst of the morning hustle. The ride was slow and full of purpose, as if watching the passers-by was part of the tour, a tiny stage production of regular Cambodians going about their day.

There wasn't much to Siem Reap once you got past the hotels. The buildings were mainly one or two-story family dwellings, many of which boasted a store front, eatery, or some other service at ground level. Repair shops for cars, bikes, and motorcycles were a popular choice of business; not surprising given the condition of the roads. Most were wide strips of dirt flattened by the relentless stream of foot and auto traffic, riven by potholes big enough for geese to swim in if it rained enough. Though the main artery through town had been pavement at some point, the earth below had long since swallowed it up. The scattered patches of asphalt that remained now littered the road as obstacles to be avoided. I could only imagine what one of them would do to this little dirt bike I was on.

Life for the people here was one of poverty, and the line was low. Whole families crowded onto Vespas, young men pulled enormous carts on their backs, and countless children pranced about shoeless in the dirt. The streets were shared by cars, trucks, bicycles, animals, and pedestrians all going this way and that in a kind of barely-controlled chaos. I wondered how often something terrible happened on the road. I wondered where the nearest hospital was, if there were doctors on call, and how long it would take the police to respond. Was there even a number to call if someone needed an ambulance? It was a potent reminder of what a lucky son of a bitch I was – a child of late 20th century America. My life was that of a prince. What the hell did I know about poverty?

My knuckles whitened around the rails as we banked a hard left onto a much smoother road. A river appeared on our right. The stillness of it reflected the trees on the other side, though the edges were overrun by lily pads and other nameless green things. Several yards ahead it made a dramatic turn to the right, the far bank ending abruptly as the water wound its way behind it.

We turned right again at a stop sign no one took seriously. The river followed us again in a nice, straight line on the right-hand side.

Wait a sec... since when do rivers change course at 90-degree angles?

Light bulbs blinked on in my head as the line of trees on the far bank yielded to massive stone walls. Distant spires I recognized from countless photos shot to the sky behind them. This wasn't a river at all – it was a *moat*. I turned around and gave Celine a jubilant thumbs up, just before we drifted to a halt beside a great stone bridge that crossed the water. Beyond lay the incomparable site of Angkor Wat.

The cooling breeze vanished and the climate of the region collapsed on us in full force. Sweat flowed in buckets from every crevice, rendering me a sticky, stinky little monkey. Thank the Lord I'd bathed in SPF 50 before leaving the hotel.

this heat is unbear—

*Look. Where. We are.*

The bridge must have been at least 200 yards long, and wide enough for a dozen people to cross side by side. Its dark, ancient-looking stonework crumbled in several spots at the edges, while statues of beasts, faces long disintegrated by erosion, kept a silent vigil on either side. By then the sound of the street had faded and an impossible silence had descended on the place. Or was it just in my head? We stepped onto the bridge and started across.

The hundred or so visitors that morning drifted quietly towards the south gate at the far end of the bridge, where a tall, flat-topped tower stood over a tiny black rectangle that must have been the doorway. Pillar after pillar of mighty gray sandstone stretched towards the jungle far off to the left and right, supporting an open-air hallway that was easily a thousand yards across. My hands tightened around my camera and went to work.

The human trickle nudged us along until we reached the gate and passed underneath a dark, narrow archway. As we stepped across the threshold, an enormous courtyard opened up before us with a suddenness that was almost alarming. My jaw dropped. The enormous central temple was now fully visible, its five lofty spires leaping towards the sky and dominating the vista with an overwhelming hypnotic power.

"Holy shit," Celine gasped. It was like a master chef had lifted the cover off some magnificent dish prepared just for us.

The causeway continued on for what seemed like a mile, cutting through the center of a vast, grassy expanse that could fit a million people. A bit further ahead a pair of small stone buildings flanked the path forward. Behind them, great rectangular basins of still water served as immense reflecting pools. We made our way to the one on the left. The image of the temple beyond was mirrored with perfect clarity, framed by palm trees in front and the morning sun blazing behind.

"Are we impressed yet?" I asked.

Celine's eyes didn't budge from where they were transfixed on the monstrosity before us.

"Amazing," she whispered.

Angkor Wat was constructed in the Hindu tradition in homage to Vishnu, one of the supreme deities, and designed to represent the five sacred peaks of Mount Meru. In both Hinduism and Buddhism, this holy mountain is the center of the entire cosmos, the known and the unknown, and the dwelling place of all divine beings. It was an ambitious thing to attempt the recreation of such a place using mere stone and mortar. A touch of hubris, even. But the Khmer did not disappoint – if ever there was a building to reflect the vastness of all creation, surely it was this one.

"Let's go inside."


We climbed the stairs to the second level and began a counter-clockwise sweep. The vast colonnade was open on the external side and looked down onto the courtyard where we'd entered. On the other side, the wall was covered with bas-reliefs depicting various themes in Hinduism. Epic struggles between gods and demons raged across the stone all around us, the likenesses of celestial figures decorating nearly every surface. The scenes followed us everywhere, telling the great mythological stories of the era.

Halfway across the gallery stood a large *gopura* (entrance building) that led us out onto the grassy, second-level terrace. Straight ahead another set of stairs, taller and steeper than before, climbed the monstrous wall surrounding the third level. We made a quick circle around the terrace then headed up.

The third level was far smaller than the last, and almost completely enclosed. The surrounding gallery no longer opened towards the outside. Stone dominated in all directions while the bas-reliefs continued along every wall, column, and doorway. The visitor-per-square-foot ratio increased dramatically on the terrace here, which was paved entirely by stone. The scenery was commanded, however, by a wide, ridiculously steep staircase that ascended to the fourth and final level, where the temple's five magnificent spires stabbed the sky. Dozens of heads were turned upwards as visitors nervously watched their friends and relatives climb up and down again. There was nothing to prevent a 45-degree head-over-heels tumble that would smart something fierce the next morning.

I noticed only then that Celine had vanished. I circled the terrace to find her and let her know I was going to the top. No luck. She'd probably already gone ahead of me. The Gremlin grumbled as I stood at the bottom of the stairs and looked up – he was not cool with heights. I took a deep breath, sent my mind to Krabi, and began to climb.

The top gallery was once again open to the outside. From this fourth and final level I gazed all the way back to the outer walls and the moat beyond, its true size laid plain at this distance by the tiny specs of tourists buzzing about like brightly-colored fleas. The central tower could be approached from the four cardinal directions via four sets of stairs leading up from the terrace. It climbed heavenward in cylindrical tiers, the perimeter of each was adorned with countless statues that once may have been gods, monsters, and men, but whose features had been smoothed into nothing by centuries of erosion. Nonetheless, what remained challenged one to believe it was wrought by beings of flesh and bone. It was, in both size and splendor, mountainous.

A group of four or five tourists were sprawled out on the floor at its base, either passed out from exhaustion or just enjoying a respite in the shadow of the tower. Normally I'd be irked by such a lack of respect at a holy site (not to mention the eyesore), but it was so friggin' hot that my empathy cut through my vexation. Perhaps the presence of the Buddha had rubbed off on me. We'd passed more and more statues of him on the way to the top, and up here they were everywhere. But why were they all missing their heads? One or two could be put down to some freak accident or careless visitors, but *all* of them? Very odd.

I found Celine sitting in a shady spot on the gallery wall, her legs hanging over the side as she pondered the horizon. The roof of the third gallery below looked close enough to spit on, appearing as a great stone levee keeping an ocean of green at bay as the thick canopy jungle of the countryside crashed against it like a tide. There were neither blue skies nor white clouds above or beyond, only the dull, gray haze of mind-boggling humidity. I plopped down next to her to share the view, drenched in sweat, completely drained, and gulping for breath through the stifling air.

The surrounding wilderness was endless – drop me in the middle of it and I wouldn't last a day. What a merciless terrain, teeming with thorns, vines, and venom, every square meter offering a dozen ways to meet your doom. To eke out a life in the deep jungle required the kind of iron will I couldn't muster in a dozen lifetimes. The Khmer built an empire in it. What a well-deserved mindblow that old Franciscan friar must have felt as the first Westerner to stumble upon this place. There he was, trudging through the jungle for months and months thinking he's on a holy quest to bring the light of Christendom to the poor godless savages of Indochina, when suddenly the trees open up and the majesty of Angkor is revealed in all its glory. A lethal dose of reality delivered right to the nuts – these "savages" had accomplished something that medieval Europe couldn't begin to rival. I would have loved to have a beer with him on that day.

Celine was absorbed in her own world as well, contemplating whatever she was apt to contemplate while astride one of the wonders of civilization. There she sat, amidst an impossibly picturesque backdrop, this darling with whom I'd shared this remarkable journey to Japan and beyond. I sat there trying to read her mind when a strange thought occurred to me.

I'd become best friends with a mystery.

This girl hadn't even existed before I awoke from that lousy nap at the airport two years ago to find her sitting there, placed in that exact spot at that exact moment by whatever trick of fate had conspired to shake up my life with her presence. I'd learned nothing about the town she'd grown up in, the school she went to, if she'd been popular, what sports she'd played, if she got along with her parents, if she'd ever had her heart broken, if she'd ever fractured a rib, gotten into a fist fight, or spent the night in jail, if she was a straight-A student or career slacker, or if she had a pet tarantula named

Mr. Pibbles. I'd picked up only a handful of factoids from conversations we'd had, none of which were ever a deep dive into her past. I only knew she was from somewhere near Ottawa, loved swimming, had a brother with a motorcycle, was a bit of a stoner, spent some time in West Africa, and was hell-bent on a career in the Canadian Defense Department.

It was the same with just about everyone else I'd befriended out here. We all met as strangers in a foreign land. None of us had grown up together, so our relationships didn't have that foundation to build on. What we did have, however, was the shared experience of living abroad, and all the joys, pains, terrors, and triumphs that came with it. It was a rare species of friendship, based on a specific time and place, burning extra brightly but for a painfully short time. Expat friends don't even have the luxury of drifting apart – the countdown just ends one day and we go our separate ways, the rug pulled out from under our feet. I left pieces of my soul behind with Glenn and Maya. Celine would be no exception. Hell, I'd probably miss her most of all. She was the Scarecrow to my Dorothy.

"You realize I know almost nothing about you?" It fell out of my mouth almost as soon as I'd thought it.

She turned and looked me dead in the eye, as if sizing me up for the very first time. A little smirk appeared on her mouth and she turned her gaze back to the jungle.

"Does that matter?" she asked.

I opened my mouth to respond, but nothing came out.

"C'mere, I want a picture." She whipped out her camera, threw her arm around my neck, and pulled me in for a selfie. Back in those primitive days you had to wait to see how your pictures turned out, so she snapped a bunch to be on the safe side. Then she turned her head, her face inches from mine. Beads of sweat glistened on her forehead, complimenting the insect repellant and sunblock of which we both reeked. Celine had blue eyes.

"You wanna get to know me better?" she asked seductively, biting her lip.

"I think that would be hazardous to my health," I said.

"Come on!" she urged, scooting even closer. "I bet there's a thousand places around here we could shag and no one would see us." She gripped my knee and flashed her eyebrows.

My bullshit detector beeped fast and loud. "Madam," I declared. "I do believe this constitutes sexual harassment."

Her deadpan broke and she snorted a laugh. "In your dreams, lover boy."

"In *my* dreams?"

She clapped me on the back and stood up again. "Tell you what. I'll send you a signed copy of my biography when I'm rich and famous." She turned and hopped back onto the terrace.


Two hours and many photos later we decided we'd conquered the place. On the way back down we barely even noticed the monk standing quietly next to one of the headless buddhas. He couldn't have been more than eight years old; in another life he could have been one of my students. I fought the urge to rub his shaved head (a huge no-no for a monk) as he smiled at us, inviting us to light a stick of incense. We accepted and I dropped the few coins I had left in my pocket into the small collection plate to the side. His smile widened and he bowed to us in a wordless *namaste*.

Something odd caught my attention as we crossed the third terrace once again. A nearby section of wall displayed one of the many carved images of dancing *apsaras* (ethereal beings), only these ones appeared under a mighty constellation of stars shining above. I hadn't come across that particular design before, so my curiosity was tickled. About three feet from the wall we stopped and an ominous chill shuddered through my sternum.

"Oh my God," Celine said in a disgusted voice.

The stars weren't stars. They were bullet holes.

I suddenly had a theory about the headless buddhas. I'd learned long ago about how the Khmer Rouge had torn the country apart in the '70s during its reign of horror and genocide. Still, it was hard to believe they would bring that madness here. Angkor seemed untouchable. Celine was walking away again before I could say a word, refusing to let her mood be sullied by one of history's monsters. I followed her gladly.

When we reached to the front gate again I took another long look behind me in quiet gratitude – I still couldn't believe a wretch like me had beheld such a place. Turning at last to face the loud, busy road was like stepping back through the wardrobe with the Pevensie children, the enchanted snows of Narnia yielding to a bunch of dusty fur coats back in the real world.

We had two other high-priority missions that day – Angkor Thom and Ta Prohm. Neither of these temples compared to Angkor Wat in size, but both were equally wondrous to behold. Rather than five lofty spires, Angkor Thom sported a multitude of smaller towers around a monolithic central one. Into these were carved enormous smiling faces that looked out in each cardinal direction. They were as tall as a man and just as wide, yet had an uncanny ability to sneak up on a person around corners and through doorways. And the detail on them was remarkably well-preserved. Either the place had just been lucky through the ages or there had been some top-quality restoration efforts in recent years. If monsters had been carved into the rock instead, the place would be downright terrifying.

Celine and I made our way through from the north. The gate at the far end was at least fifty feet high and crowned by a solitary spire atop a massive archway, adorned once again by a giant face in each direction. A huge stone bridge led away from it, bordered by rows of mysterious stone figures looking ominously towards the center of the bridge as if in warning. On the left, stern-faced gods. On the right, scowling demons. Some had been restored after having their heads removed, while others could have been untouched for a millennium. It was straight out of *Indiana Jones.*

Our pilots were waiting for us at the far end of the bridge and we were off again. Our final stop, Ta Prohm, was unique among all the sites at Angkor – it was left completely unrestored. The idea was to show exactly what they'd found when the place was "re-discovered" after being abandoned for hundreds of years. This provided visitors with a glimpse of what happens to a stone temple when left to the mercy of the jungle for five or six centuries.

Even the biggest sandstone blocks won't stop a

determined tree once it's made up its mind to start growing. Ta Prohm evidenced this in spectacular detail. The jungle didn't grow up around the temple or push it to the side, it grew *through* it. Enormous trees wrapped around the outer walls like tentacles before rocketing to the canopy above. Their trunks emerged from the earth as big as a Volkswagen, gradually becoming thinner as they wriggled their way upwards in reality-defying twists and turns around the stone. The visual effect was different depending on the kind of tree. In some places roots and trunks exploded through the stone with devastating effect, leaving the shattered remains of walls strewn about its base, while in another spot the growth was so straight and clean it looked like an enormous potted plant. The "stranglers" were the real gems. These were a parasitic species of fig that survived by attacking a host tree, casting its sinuous roots around its victim and swallowing it whole. The tree inside would then die, leaving only the skeletal structure surrounding it. They looked more like spider webs than tree roots.

At that time people could still explore Ta Prohm freely without boundaries, ropes, or boardwalks. Knowing this couldn't possibly last, Celine and I took full advantage. The roots were big enough to climb in several places, and the dark, fantastical aura of the temple's inner corridors made it catnip for the imagination. Monsters surely lurked around every corner of this accursed place, guarding the final resting place of Blugbor the Destroyer in the catacombs below. So, naturally, it was up to me to discover the tomb, break the curse, and liberate the village. The townsfolk were depending on me.

"What the hell are you doing?" Celine laughed as I

whipped around the corner, finger pistols aimed for a headshot.

"Shhhh!" I spat as I glanced side to side, scanning for enemies.

"It's kinda creepy in here," she said.

"That's Blugbor's doing."

The sun was low in the sky when our limbs reached the brink of collapse. Neither of us had ever felt such intense heat and we couldn't focus on anything but cooling off somehow. The mass of gray clouds growing in the distance confirmed it was time to call it a day.

We got back to the hotel and fell in the pool. The cool water was like rain in the desert. Then we dragged our aching bones over to the restaurant and gobbled down some spicy chicken and rice. Life crept back into to our bodies. So, naturally, we decided to find ourselves a bar and kill our brains instead. As luck would have it, there was one a block away. The evening ended unceremoniously, the two of us nodding off after the second-and-a-half Singapore Sling.

I woke up around 1:00 a.m. thinking a herd of lemmings was stampeding on the roof directly overhead. After listening in semi-delirium for a while, the sharper part of my brain concluded that it was just the rain. A serious, furious rain.

"Well, I guess we're sleeping in," was my last thought before drifting back to sleep.

The rain continued throughout the early morning, significantly limiting our options for our last day at Angkor. Han and Solo were supposed to meet us again, but surely they'd assume we'd want to wait until the storm passed before venturing out again. We ate breakfast inside, watching the deluge in the street with hearts that would have been heavier but for the success of the previous day. It showered in sheets, straight down, loud, and relentless.

Then it stopped.

Within three minutes the street was full of people again, not an umbrella to be seen. Assuming this was just a mad dash before the next downpour, we nursed our second and third cups of coffee with all the urgency of a tree sloth. How little we knew. Our eyes widened at the sudden arrival of clear skies and a bright sun, and now we were wasting precious time sitting here like idiots. The sloth mutated into a squirrel.

As if on cue, Han and Solo walked through the front door. Celine jumped up from her seat and waved to them.

"Hey! Perfect timing! Did you just get here?"

Han walked over and bid us good morning. "Yes, we were just across the street."

"Awesome! Should we go now or do you think it will rain again?"

"No, we can go now," Solo replied. "It won't rain again today."

And with that, we were off again. We'd planned to make a bunch of short visits to the many smaller temples we'd passed by the day before, then have one last look at Angkor Wat to wrap it all up. But after the fourth of fifth one we found ourselves succumbing to "temple fatigue," an acute condition where stone temples all start to look the same regardless of their splendor. I could tell Celine was thinking what I was thinking.

"Should we just go back to Angkor Wat now?" I asked.

you'll regret it!

*Overruled.*

"Yes!" my Canadian friend shouted. "Let's do it."

The morning rain had brought in cooler air than the day before, so this time around was more mellow. There were also far fewer people around. We took our sweet time exploring the various nooks and crannies we hadn't noticed yesterday – Angkor Wat was even more massive than we'd realized. We went around back and into the trees behind the temple, following several overgrown paths towards the moat and stopping often to take artsy-fartsy photos in pretty spots, of which there were heaps. We chatted with one or two westerners we met and took a few candid snapshots of people in various states of awe. Before long I'd exhausted my film, even the old black and white backup rolls. We took our second climb to the summit at a snail's pace, clockwise this time, with an extra focus on exploring the wall carvings and other details.

Running out of film freed up my hands to explore the textures of the stone itself, and unlocked my other senses as well. I shut my eyes to let the other four take the wheel for a while. I ran my palms along the bas-reliefs as we crossed the galleries, gently caressing the mythologies of creation as they played out about my fingertips. I breathed in the inescapable aroma of earth and jungle, punctuated all the more by the fresh rainfall hours before. At the risk of appearing a lunatic, I leaned into the wall a bunch of times to have a whiff of the stone. The smell reminded me of old books. Aside from the rhythmic crunch of tiny stones grinding underneath Celine's footfalls behind me, the only sound to be heard was the dull, steady hum of insects off to the right, interrupted by the occasional bird calling out to a lover. The symphony of the forest. My eyes popped back open whenever another human being approached, which I heard from a mile away.

We spent the whole afternoon there, wasting no thought on what we might have missed. There's nothing repetitive about visiting a place like Angkor Wat a second time – it's an opportunity cost well worth paying. We left with the sunset, minds blown all over again.


We ended up at last night's pub to bask in the afterglow of another extraordinary day. It had cooled down mightily with the setting of the sun, so we took our Mai Tais outside. We mused upon how much we liked Han and Solo and loathed the Khmer Rouge. We swapped funny stories about our (former) students and made fun of some super-loud Scottish tourists who came in after us. At some point, the conversation stopped and we just sat there pondering the afternoon. I twisted my torso to the left and right to stretch my spine with a series of pops before sinking into my chair, resting the back of my neck on the top of it. The joy on Celine's face was contagious.

"I'm gonna miss this sooo much," she said. "Traveling is the greatest thing ever!"

My hand clutched my heart. "Aww, I'll miss you too, sweetie pie!"

"You know you will."

It was true. This was probably the last drink we'd ever have together. I looked down at my glass and tried to come up with a proper toast for the occasion, but my mind was blank.

"I'm so glad we got to do this," Celine said. "After like a month back in Canada I'm gonna be like, *Blech, get me the hell out of here!*"

"Well, yeah," I replied. "I mean, it's Canada."

"Ha! Whatever, loser. We both know you wish you were Canadian." She broke into her own massive stretch, bending backwards and throwing out her arms like an upside-down cat. She then deflated into a contented blob.

"Know what you'll do first when you get home?" I asked.

"Oh, I am going straight to my parents' lake house and spending the rest of the summer just sitting in the sun, eating Lebanese food, and swimming every day."

"Your parents' *lake house*?"

"Yep."

"You sicken me."

"Yeah, it's super nice," she beamed, not a trace of guilt on her face. "What'll you do?"

"No real plans," I said with a shrug. "Probably just go back home, sit on my ass for a while and then try to get my life on track."

"Screw that," she spat. "Your life is just fine. If plans aren't your thing, then you should just keep going. Travel for as long as you possibly can. You can teach English pretty much anywhere if you don't mind living cheap."

I nodded. "Believe me, I've thought about it. I don't

think I could teach kids again, though."

"Hell, no. No more children. Fucking brats."

It always made me laugh to hear Celine talk about her students that way. I had to admit though, I kind of missed mine. Some of them, anyway.

"To the brats!" I declared, raising my glass. "May the damage we've done fade quickly!"

"Cheers!" she answered. We swallowed the dregs our cocktails and slammed the glasses down hard. Celine's eyes drifted to something behind me.

"Allo, gecko!"

Eight hours later we were back at the airport waiting for separate flights to carry us our separate ways. We were both Japan bound, but Celine was flying back to Toronto via Tokyo. I was going to Baltimore via Osaka. Her flight was two hours after mine, so we found ourselves a diner near my departure gate and got lunch. I tried not to get emotional as we talked emptily about this and that. She loathed long goodbyes and was a fervent believer in getting them over with as quickly as possible. Dragging them out only made them worse. I saw the wisdom in this, of course, and tried to get on that wavelength as we spent our last minutes together. It wasn't easy.

Suddenly the intercom announced the boarding of my flight. I took a deep breath, dropped my hands to my lap, and forced a smile as I looked at my friend.

"Oh, God," she muttered weakly. She thumped her elbows down on the table, clapping her hands over her mouth as tears forced their way through her cast-iron façade.

She quickly steeled herself, cleared her throat and stood up. My own eyes began to float as a line from my favorite book popped into my head.

*Here at last, upon the shores of the sea, comes the end of our fellowship.*

We walked over to my gate, side by side in a slow silence. I stopped when we arrived, surprising myself by not laughing as Celine kept walking right on past.

"Oi," I said in my classroom voice. She looked around for a moment before realizing she'd left me behind. I pointed to the gate to my left. "This is me."

Without a word Celine dropped her bags, ran to me at full speed, and leapt into my arms, wrapping her legs around my backside for a full-on jump 'n' hug.

"Really, Celine? In front of everyone?" I gave her a spin as my heart melted.

She was smiling again when I put her down, her voice shaky but strong. "You have to keep in touch, okay? Email me and tell me what's going on with you."

"I will if you will," I said. "And do let me know when you're Prime Minister!"

I handed my boarding pass to the nice lady and stepped over the threshold, then took a final look back. Celine blew me a kiss, turned, and walked off to conquer the world. The first and mightiest of my cabal had at last departed, this titan among Canadians, her blonde ponytail bopping unapologetically as she faded into the mass of people in transit.

Reality transformed with each echoing step down the jetway. After two years, this most peculiar and wondrous life chapter had concluded much as it had begun, the roller coaster returning to the launch pad after a short, dizzying ride. Whatever future lay that before me had not yet begun, and for the second time in my life I found myself adrift in a limbo between worlds. My thoughts swayed like a seesaw in the breeze, back and forth between *okonomi yaki* and Taco Bell, the *shinkansen* and the D.C. metro, my expat allies and my old high school crew. The sickness of leaving was at equilibrium with the excitement of arriving anew, and the Gremlin was quiet. I popped in my earphones and reclined my seat. For the next fifteen hours over the Pacific I floated through the ether of the unknown, without the foggiest idea of what would come next.

That would have scared me once. I couldn't help but smile at that.

# LIMBO REVISITED

Detroit Metropolitan Airport was at its loveliest on the afternoon of September 17, 2004. The plane had touched down hard and jolted me out of my booze-induced pseudo-sleep just in time for the flight attendant's "Welcome to America" spiel to bore a hole or two into my skull. I had a connecting flight to D.C. in three hours and was free to wander the airport in search of new and exciting ways to do nothing. I popped on my sunglasses, threw up my hood, and clenched my toes to dull the pins and needles that attacked me with a blast of cold air from the terminal.

A barrage of stars and stripes tattooed every available white space – a residual effect of Iraq War II, no doubt, now in its second year. The ungodly fluorescence all around made me wince through the tinted lenses as I breathed in the stale, dry air.

The Gremlin grumbled and bared its filthy teeth, itching to get in a few choice words to mark the occasion. It didn't get the chance, because just then a curious phenomenon occurred.

I heard familiar voices off to my right. No, it couldn't be. I didn't know anyone in Detroit, did I? I heard them again, dead ahead this time.

A couple and their two children chatted about Halloween costumes as they waited to board. The older kid wanted the younger kid to dress up as the dead girl from *The Ring* who climbs out of the TV and kills people, but the mother was having none of it. I'd never seen these people in my life and couldn't care less about what they did for Halloween, yet I had to fight down an inexplicable urge to go talk to them. Was my mind playing tricks? Did I know them?

Nope, definitely strangers. I gave them one last mental scan in spite of myself before snapping out of it and continuing on my way. Every word of their conversation registered loud and clear until I passed out of earshot. Then the pins and needles returned in force, no amount of toe clenching doing away with them this time.

I walked towards my gate and it happened again, this time with a couple of bros talking about football. What the hell was going on? I didn't know them either, yet some magnetic force drew me to their chatter. I just couldn't tune any of it out. I wasn't listening to anyone, but I heard *everyone*, and not just as background noise. Whenever I passed by close enough to hear someone, my brain would latch onto what they were saying, jumping around from person to person depending on who was talking loudest. And they were all talking to *me*.

My eyes darted around like flies trying to find the source of the conversations, as if it were imperative that I acknowledge them. It was like the volume of the English language had been turned to max and my ears were made of glass, ready to shatter from the vibration.

these people need to shut the f—

*Headphones. Now.*

I stuffed them in my ears and felt better immediately, breathing out a toxic fume of tension that had no earthly explanation. My shoulders relaxed and my head rolled forward, thanking the gods for the technological miracle that was the Discman.

But then my vision started doing its own wacky thing. The conversations were muted, but now I kept thinking I *recognized* everyone. Different versions of *"Wait, isn't that..."* played over and over again in my addled brain as I waded through the river of fellow Americans. An entire airport full of people, every one of them connected to me in some way my mind strove to define. Childhood friends stood in line at the Burger King, classmates mingled at the bar, distant cousins emerged from the bathrooms. I was too bugged out to even look at the Dunkin' Donuts. I forced my eyes to my shoes and kept walking. Arriving at last to my gate I planted myself in a corner seat by the window, jittery from the recent assault on my senses.

Welcome to reverse culture shock – a temporary but unsettling condition in which what was once strange is normal and what was once normal is strange. In my case, hearing my mother tongue in such heavy doses was enough to make my brain do cartwheels. I must have been gone longer than I'd realized.

I didn't recognize them until we'd practically collided. The reunion was merry enough, albeit a tad surreal and dulled by exhaustion. I was able to get my arms around mum more easily than I remembered. The South Beach Diet had done its work well. Dad's hair had gone from gray to white since I'd last seen him and he was actually wearing his glasses. Noting my haggard appearance and borderline psychotic behavior, they concluded that I needed to hit the sack. As we walked towards the baggage claim, my mind bounced between random conversations as it had done all afternoon.

A blast of exasperation shot through my teeth – why hadn't I thought of it before? I closed my eyes, dove deep down, and summoned the orb with a desperate fury. My head rolled to the left before snapping hard to the right, as if I were flinging leeches from my ears, and the voices died down a little. I still heard them, but they were no longer stabbing my brain with impunity. However, it was tough to hold myself in this state given the relentlessness of the barrage. The orb came and went, drawn into my mind's eye by sheer force of will only to be struck down time and again by its attackers. A game of mental whack-a-mole. I just wasn't sure which end of the mallet I was on.

Mum's voice was loud and cheerful. "You seem distracted. A penny for your thoughts!" This was one of the quirky things she was prone to say.

they wouldn't underst—

*Be nice.*

The parents listened intently as I told them about the phenomenon in Detroit, which continued to torment me here in IAD as we waited for the baggage carousel to awaken. I tried to stay lucid enough to answer their questions, but couldn't manage for long. I was happy to see them and certainly had a tale or two to tell, but trans-Pacific flights have a way of sapping the life out of a person. By the time my bags appeared the only voices I heard were once again the dull, distant ones of random passers-by.

Finally we stepped through the doors and my Vans kissed asphalt. The bright lights vanished, replaced by a blissfully overcast early evening. The voices yielded to the music of distant jet engines and heavy traffic all around us. We found the car and I flopped into the back seat. Dad turned the engine over and the radio came to life with earth-shattering power, Rush Limbaugh mid-sentence in some tirade about Hillary Clinton. I heard it just long enough to taste battery acid in my mouth.

Someone slapped the radio off and my body deflated again. The quiet was magnificent.

"Is there anything special you want to eat?" was the last thing I heard as I faded to black in the bosom of the first comfortable seat I'd had in nearly thirty hours.

"Hummus?"

For the next two weeks the fridge was overflowing with the stuff.

It took just four days to cross everything off my "things to do back home" list. I gorged myself on Taco Bell, mac 'n' cheese, and this new thing called Chipotle. I shot pool in Dupont Circle and got sloshed at the old watering holes in Adams Morgan, all the while endangering countless lives dusting the cobwebs off my driving skills. Most importantly, or so I thought, I was brought up to speed on what had been going on in the lives of my nearest and dearest.

But all conversations eventually turned to the Iraq War. My friends spoke of it with an energy too intense for me to return in kind, hesitating little in offering their two cents on the matter. I should have been all ears. It was, after all, the most burning global issue of the new century and I reviled the American penchant for war as much as the next guy. But I just couldn't identify with this one – it didn't ignite the same fire in me as it did in my countrymen. In fact, I was sick to death of hearing about it. All I wanted to do was bare my soul about how badly I missed the place I'd just come from. Was that so selfish?

Plus, it wasn't like I was all there to begin with. "You seem pretty out of it" was something I heard a lot those first few days back home. I found myself staring at random people at restaurants, not drinking my drinks, and missing the punchline of too many jokes. I drove around just for the sake of driving and parked in the furthest corners of the lots just to enjoy the extra walk. I stood awestruck before Planet Boyardee and the Great Wall of Kellogg's at my local Safeway. And I ate *everything* with chopsticks now. I had my quirks before, but there was evidence I'd finally crossed into the realm of just plain weird.

On the fifth morning I awoke to the gaping silence of

suburbia, not at all familiar now, and for a second I didn't know where I was. My esophagus vibrated with a long, lifeless groan as I pushed myself into a sitting position, eyes clamped shut and unwilling to face the cruel light of day. My head swam across the Pacific as memories of Japan came rushing in like locusts. I sat at the edge of the bed for a long while, seriously considering the possibility that I'd just been unplugged from the Matrix. I might as well have dreamt the whole damn thing.

I opened my eyes and barely recognized the room I'd slept in for half my life. I was back in my parents' basement, the same corner of the same world I'd escaped from twenty-five months ago. Nothing had followed me back through the looking glass. I'd come full circle. But the circle was broken.

coming back was a big mist—

*No.*

I stepped out of the bedroom and wandered around the house, going from room to room as if I were in the market to buy the place. Every inch of my childhood home should have triggered all kinds of memories, but nothing was registering. It was all distant and two-dimensional. The closet full of old toys, the big bathroom with the walk-in shower, the '70s-style wood paneling in the den, even the pool table I'd worshipped in high school. None of it was mine anymore. It all belonged to that kid who used to live here, and he never came back from Japan. Wherever home was, it wasn't here. It wasn't anywhere near here.

The hunter green JanSport backpack that had followed

me everywhere stank of a hundred different airports, hotels, taxis, and closets whose aroma it had slowly absorbed throughout the course of its tumultuous life. Good ol' green backpack. It was the first thing my hands went for when I finally decided to unpack.

I reached in and yanked out my laptop with too much force, nearly sending it careening like a frisbee. It awoke from its mechanical slumber and started up right where I'd left off. I'd been tinkering with my beta account on this funky new "Gmail" thing when I'd last closed it.

In my inbox sat a solitary email from Celine, sent this morning at 7:07 a.m. There was a single line of text:

HEY, LOSER! I'M GOING TO PARIS.

The neighbors could have heard me laughing. Celine's signature greeting had always nudged my funny bone, but today it was magic. An alien transmission from a distant galaxy. It was the first sign I hadn't lost everything when I left Japan, an indestructible relic of a bygone age. Something of that past life would endure, even if it was just the occasional email from a smart-alecky Canadian.

But something stirred deeper down. I looked again. Paris.

jealous?

*Inspired.*

My forehead hit the spacebar as the awful thing lingering in my belly for the past five days vanished. I stood up again and looked out the window. I knew what I wanted. Maybe I just needed a friend to remind me. I bit my fist and sent a telepathic message into the ether with everything I could muster.

"I miss you already, stupid girl."

Her fingers may have typed about Paris, but Celine's words carried an altogether different message:

*You'll be fine. Just GO.*


Suddenly it all seemed ludicrous. *Of course* I was going to keep traveling. Hell, I'm not sure I could have stopped even if I'd wanted to, given my condition. I hadn't received any official diagnosis, but all signs indicated I'd suffered a lethal bite from what's commonly known as the "travel bug." Symptoms include a shrunken world, reckless curiosity, and an insatiable desire to avoid the motherland at all costs. When it progresses to its advanced stages it doesn't matter where you go, or for how long, as long as you remain mobile. And the disease must run its course. It becomes an entire identity, an ever-transient lifestyle, forged by the insane belief that it's the only one that will ever make any sense.

But it *did* make sense. It made perfect, geometric sense to me – one of the few things in life that did. Time was short and the wide world wasn't all that wide. Its spooky mask had fallen off and the face of the earth underneath was cherubic. It had become small, familiar, and welcoming, wanting nothing more than for me to spend my days trotting it from end to end. The opportunity was there to be seized, just as it had been on that monumental day back in college.

No... not like then. Nothing like then. I didn't get some random email with a limited-time offer. There was no high-pressure interview, no recruitment process, no take-it-or-leave-it sense of immediacy. I wasn't out of options and I didn't need to escape some terrible fate that would otherwise befall me. I'd spent the last two years enduring the crucible of teaching and was now armed to the teeth with that experience. It was a weapon that now hung securely from my belt – the sword with which I could carve out a life anywhere on Earth where there was a demand for English.

And if teaching was my sword, meditation was undoubtedly my shield. Barring some catastrophic act of God or violence, there was no situation I couldn't handle while I had control over my mind. None of the hesitation and self-doubt of those first few weeks in Nagaoka remained. I was immune to that now. Loneliness was no longer a thing, and the words "waste" and "time" didn't go together. The Gremlin was no longer a worthy adversary, he was my obedient little pet. Sure, he'd pop out of his cage from time to time, but I knew just how to slam him back in.

Besides, it wasn't like I was going to bugger off and join a tribe of warrior nomads in the Sahara. I knew my limits. Meditation doesn't impair judgment, it fortifies the being. Living abroad would be effortless with this power at my command.


One night in very early 2005, I opened up the journal I'd kept. It reeked of *nag champa* incense and cannabis, but the pages were still nice and crisp. I could tell which entries were made in the throes of intoxication, revealed by both excessive emotionality and ungodly penmanship. Those were always good for a chortle. I flipped to the beginning and read the entry I made the night I arrived in Nagaoka.

September 2, 2002

I have to start WORK tomorrow. In the big picture, I've come to the point right before retirement and death:

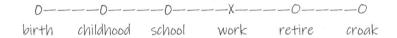

I mean, WHAT THE FUCK?!? What the hell is happening to me? Wasn't I *just* worrying about entering the third grade? Is this how people grow old? Damn man my mood just turned sour. A bit, anyway. Will I be retired before I even realize that I worked? Will I die before I even realize that I lived?

I stared at it in disbelief. That poor kid was so narrow-minded and pessimistic I barely recognized him. What a sad notion to see your entire life laid out in a single, unbreakable line, the track beneath the express train to the grave. And to feel helpless enough to believe it. Where on earth did cynicism of that magnitude come from? I wanted to reach out to my younger self and simultaneously hug him, lecture him, and smack him upside the head.

*Young man, you drew that line all wrong. It loops and turns and breaks and scatters and goes up, down, sideways and all around, here and there and who knows where. You just don't know it yet. Now pick it up and bend it.*

Who knew my time in Japan would dispel the ultimate myth I was brought up on – that there was one path to happiness, and to deviate from it meant indigence and ruin. How many of us still see it all through that lens, our lives as a one-way road through the desert, the truth only revealing itself in a horrible moment of crisis when it's already too late? One random email in college saved me from that, and I very nearly deleted it without a look.

Divine intervention is tough to dismiss sometimes.

It would have been so easy to stay whatever course my life was on before that day, no matter how unhappy it made me. Christ, how many other opportunities had I botched because the Gremlin started howling? How much of living life had I talked myself out of over the years?

"I wish I'd done something like that!" was a common response when I told people where I'd been the last two years. The words fly past me like bullets. I think of all my almost-were futures and this luckiest of bastards is overwhelmed with gratitude. My faith in fate is restored.

# ONWARD AND SOUTHWARD

A few days later I found myself in my brother's old bedroom, rummaging through the assortment of abused paperbacks and other nerdy stuff he never let me touch. There was no shortage of maps, atlases, and other geographic reference materials to contemplate this floating pebble we live on, including, of course, a half-dozen globes of differing sizes and colors. There was one I knew inside and out from those halcyon days we tossed it around the house with all the other toys we mangled. It had always endeared me with its vibrant hues and little bumps where mountain ranges lay, and for the challenge of saying "Union of Soviet Socialist Republics" three times fast without messing up. Names like Peking, Madras, and Yugoslavia gave it that added '80s charm.

I twirled the ragged old thing back and forth from Japan and the USA. Two years prior the distance between them was like the Earth to the Moon. Now it was nothing. One night in a plane and I could step out anywhere on the ball in time for breakfast. I spun it to Canada, Mexico, Ireland, India, Thailand, Cambodia, and back to Japan, tracing a line between all the countries I'd ever been to. I counted seven. Seven, out of nearly 200. Trying to visit them all was a fool's errand, of course, but come on... *seven*? Unacceptable. How could I live with myself seeing so little of this place when it was all so accessible now?

It sure looked different upside-down with Antarctica facing up. The world's biggest desert. Holy cow, talk about isolation. *No one* goes to Antarctica. The only place that even came near it was that curly tail of South America I'd looked at countless times over the years. I even knew the name – *Tierra del Fuego* – the little triangular island that reached down across the frigid seas to point its finger at the South Pole. The Land of Fire. In my childhood I'd imagined dragons. A place shrouded in darkness, as far south as south goes, distant, mysterious, and utterly out of reach.

No longer.

*We're going south, as far as south goes. We'll walk to the end of the road until we hit the water and know the next stop is Antarctica. Then we'll decide if we want to keep going.*

can i come?

*No.*

South America was the obvious choice once I'd made it. I'd studied Spanish since I was nine and somehow still sucked at it, so it would be nice to finally become fluent. Or at least greatly improved. What better way than total immersion, right?

Chile and Argentina had for years been the two most popular destinations on the continent for ESL teachers like me, with online opinion fiercely divided over which was superior. Chile was praised for its stability, infrastructure, and incredible natural diversity. It was criticized for having lousy air and depressing winters, especially in the capital, and a particularly chewy dialect. Argentina was hailed for the arts, beef, gorgeous people, and low cost of living. It was slammed for endemic corruption, economic volatility, and disdain for North Americans. Both captivated my imagination in their own ways.

But I was choosing a place to *live*, not to just bounce around for a spell. This demanded considerations of a more pragmatic sort. What were the visa requirements? How hard was it to get a work permit? Did I need an employment contract? Can I open a bank account? Could I become a permanent resident? How long would that take? Should I even bother? The questions went on and on.

The internet was gracious enough to address many of them in detail, and there was no shortage of folks sharing their experience on this newfangled thing called "social media." To hear them talk about it, I'd have a better chance of winning the Nobel Prize than finding stable employment in Buenos Aires. Stories of shady employers and demon landlords outnumbered those in Santiago by at least three to one. There was also the little detail that the economy of Argentina had collapsed only a couple years prior, while Chile was the regional poster child for economic development. That was the straw that broke the llama's back. I chose Santiago and bought a one-way ticket.

It's a good thing, too, because that's where I met my wife.

# ACKNOWLEDGMENTS

I want to thank the following people for their support, encouragement, and tolerance of my intolerable weirdness as this whole thing came together.

Casey Reiland

Bill Fallon

Allison O'Neill

Dave Kezer

Ghazaleh Samandari

Ginelle Testa

Larry Butler

Rahul Sen Sharma

# ABOUT THE AUTHOR

Matt Niner is a veteran world traveler, the former editor of a small South American magazine, and a true believer when it comes to both meditation and comedy. He spent his twenties exploring five continents before (reluctantly) returning to his homeland to settle down for a normal life.

When he's not writing, he's either snowboarding, avoiding the gym, or hanging out with a bunch of nerds. He currently lives with his wife and two children in Germantown, Maryland.

Thanks for reading!

If you enjoyed this book and would like to help other people find it too, please consider leaving me a review on Amazon. Please do this for all the books you enjoy, since many authors depend on this kind of help to stay afloat and write their next book.

Made in United States
Orlando, FL
15 March 2025

59483475R00156